EQUIPPING
for
MINISTRY

John M. Palmer

D1565033

Gospel Publishing House
Springfield, Missouri
02-0802

This is a Sunday School Staff Training textbook. Credit for its study will be issued under Classification 5, Sunday School Department, Assemblies of God.

Library of Congress Catalog Card Number 85-80220
International Standard Book Number 0-88243-802-6
Printed in the United States of America

Contents

1

400 Ministers in a Church?

"Start where you are. Use what you have. Do what you can."

I don't recall where I first heard that, but it has profoundly influenced me for the past 10 years. In 1974, I graduated from Central Bible College and moved to Athens, Ohio, with Ty Silva, a dear friend and college classmate. We felt like a modern-day Paul and Silas coming to plant a church. Fresh from the classroom, we were short on experience, but long on enthusiasm and ready for hard work.

There was no Assemblies of God church in Athens. No one in the area knew us, and we didn't know anybody. *What do we do now?* We had been adequately prepared at CBC, and we had prayed and set some goals, but starting a church was different from what we had thought it would be.

We worked feverishly and prayed, doing all that we knew to do. One by one, God began to lead us to people who were spiritually hungry. First, Betty, then Lee and Maxine, Kevin, Randy and Cora. Our congregation began to grow. I will never forget our elation when one week's offering exceeded $100!

Were there any discouragements? Plenty! Several times I asked God to release me from this assignment and lead me to another part of His harvest field. He didn't, and now I'm glad He kept me there.

As we faithfully continued to minister by visiting, praying, following up contacts, teaching, and preaching, God was faithful to His promise in Galatians 6:9: "Let us not become weary in doing good, for at the proper time we will reap a harvest if we do not give up" (NIV).

Slowly the church became established and grew to 50, then 75, and then 100 people. Then Ty and his wife, Cina, left for another field of ministry. But God's blessing continued, and my wife, Debbie, and I experienced the joy of a growing church. Miracles of salvation and healing occurred regularly. A number of young people left to attend Bible college to formally prepare themselves for ministry. With nearly 200 in the morning worship services, we were thrilled. Our continued growth even necessitated having two morning worship services.

I was a minister, and they were the congregation. It seemed like an ideal situation. Then one day something dawned on me: I was pastoring a very nice congregation, but I was doing all the work. I did the planning, administrative work, program development, as well as much of the detail work (such as painting, running errands, and mopping floors). I found the Sunday school teachers and visited the sick and new converts. Leaving town for vacation or ministry became very difficult. The church's entire ministry rested on me, or so I thought.

I had not yet learned that the greatest untapped source of potential ministers was sitting in the pews every Sunday morning. I didn't recognize that I had one major responsibility as a pastor: "to prepare God's people for works of service" (Ephesians 4:12, NIV). At least 80 percent of this fledgling congregation had been saved under my ministry. Here was a church of loving, energetic Christians, eager to learn and serve. But I didn't know how to mobilize them. Sure, I conducted new converts classes for them and tried my best to disciple them. *But what next?*

I was trying to do everything. Only when the load became too heavy would I shift responsibilities to God's people. I would ask (or strongly encourage) them to do something for God in the church, without first determining whether they were gifted to do it. Even if they were, I did not give them proper instruction on how to do the assigned task. I had the mistaken notion that "availability means capability." Consequently, many of those who took on ministries to lighten my burden found themselves frustrated and considered themselves failures. Discouragement set in. Some of them just quietly left the church.

As their shepherd, I felt guilty and frustrated. On the one hand, I rejoiced that the Lord was bringing people into His family. On the other hand, I wondered what to do with them.

Every Christian a Minister

At that point the Lord helped me discover something that revolutionized my life and became the focus of my ministry: Every Christian is a minister. Each believer is the Lord's servant.

I am merely a minister who has been called to pastor. Jim is a minister who is a coal miner. Richard ministers as a college administrator. Tammy is a minister who is a secretary. Bub is a minister who works for the telephone company. When someone asked me how many ministers were in our church, my reply stunned him: "About 400."

Elton Trueblood stated it powerfully, "If the average church should suddenly take seriously the notion that every laymember—man or woman—is really a minister of Christ, we could have something like a revolution in a very short time."[1]

In Ephesians 4:12, Paul makes it abundantly clear. All of us are to do "the work of the ministry." Since this is true, then we are all ministers, regardless of our Bible knowledge or how long we have been serving Christ. Quite often we consider only ordained or licensed people as "the ministers." Even I did that until this truth became real to me.

After God alerted me to this concept a new thrust came to our church. About that time we were moving into a beautiful 36,000-square-foot colonial-style building adjacent to Ohio University. But now I saw that my major task was not to organize the building program, but to build people. For me, making this discovery was as important as Thomas Edison's invention of the light bulb. Without the active ministry of the congregation, the church would be unable to do its work effectively.

From Discovery to Application

Even after I made this discovery, I still faced a problem. True, each child of God is gifted. Each has something to offer in the ministry of the church. Every Christian is a minister. But how was I to lead them from that point to the point of action?

Preparing God's people for works of service is a full-time task. It is accomplished through preaching, teaching, encouraging, counseling, and helping each child of God to discover, develop, and use his spiritual gifts. We must equip and train God's people to serve, but where do we start and how do we do it?

I began to pray and read about this matter and to ask many questions. God also used men to help shape my thinking. Rob Burkhart, the Christian education director at Bethany Assembly of God in Adrian, Michigan, shared helpful insights he had discovered through a preministry course he was using in Adrian. Ken Kinghorn, a professor at Asbury Theological Seminary, also inspired me. Through their thoughts and my study of the New Testament concept of ministry, God helped me put together a practical plan.

We started with a small Sunday school class limited to between 15 and 20 members per quarter. We used a 13-week curriculum titled "Equipping for Ministry," which we had developed. One of those who completed the class, who was gifted in administration and curriculum development, helped to write a workbook to complement the course.

We established three goals for the course:

1. To have every adult in our church take this class.

2. To have all who take the class to become active in ministry.

3. To encourage those who are not yet involved to become active in ministry.

Beginning with the basic truth that each Christian is a minister, we helped the class members understand the meaning and purpose of spiritual gifts. Before a Christian will become active in the church's ministry, he must realize, "I am gifted and God can use me. He has a place of ministry for me."

The results were gratifying. By the end of 1984, 106 people had completed this course. Our records show that as of December 1984, of these 106 people, 12 no longer attended New Life Assembly but still lived in the area. Eighteen had moved away from the area. Of the 76 still attending New Life, 56 were actively involved in a ministry requiring consistent responsibility. Excluding those no longer attending New Life, 75 percent of the class members were then involved in active ministry.

Growth Through Teaching

As a direct result of this course, the church grew. In our new facility, we were conducting two morning worship services to accommodate the growth, while at the same time finalizing plans for a new 900-seat sanctuary.

But the growth went beyond just numbers. Individuals were growing. They were beginning to understand their giftedness as well as their responsibility to minister in the church. As each one exercised his or her gifts, the body was strengthened. The Holy Spirit, through Paul, put it this way: "From him [that is, Christ] the whole body, joined and held together by every supporting ligament, grows and builds itself up in love, as each part does its work" (Ephesians 4:16, NIV).

Another aspect of the resulting growth was the increasing ease with which we found people who would teach, lead youth groups, work in the nursery, or head up projects for the church. There was a constant influx of newly trained people graduating into the ministry pool.

Dare To Dream

What began as a dream became a seed, then a small plant. It sprouted into a small tree and is continuing to grow. We had tapped into the greatest source of ministerial potential: the body of believers who worshiped with us each week.

In an average congregation, at least 60 percent of the adults are not involved in active ministry. Imagine how much more evangelism, encouragement, teaching, and visitation could be taking place in and through your church if this group became mobilized for service.

As we motivate and mobilize those who are already God's children to minister for the Lord, we can more effectively reach our communities and cities for Christ. Pastor Thomas Gillespie notes that this will take place only "if the 'non-clergy' are willing to *move up*, if the 'clergy' are willing to *move over*, and if all God's people are willing to *move out*."[2]

Our commission has never changed: "Go and make disciples of all nations, baptizing them in the name of the Father and of the Son and of the Holy Spirit, and teaching them to obey everything I have commanded you. And surely I will be with you always, to the very end of the age" (Matthew 28:19,20, NIV).

If we are to fulfill this commission, we must involve every Christian in the ministry of the church. To do this, we must alert them to their usefulness in the ministry and motivate them to become involved. It is a gigantic task, but remember: Whatever God expects us to do for Him, He empowers us to do!

---

[1]Elton Trueblood, *Your Other Vocation* (New York: Harper & Brothers, 1952), p. 29.

[2]Thomas Gillespie, "The Laity in Biblical Perspective," *The New Laity*, ed. Ralph D. Bucy (Waco, TX: Word Books, 1978), p. 32.

2

It Can Happen in Your Church

A pastor's wife was teaching her primary class at vacation Bible school when something unforgettable happened. About an hour before dismissal, a new student was brought into the room.

The young boy was missing an arm. Since the class was almost over, the teacher had no opportunity to learn the background of his handicap or his state of adjustment. She was very nervous and feared that one of the children would comment on his handicap and embarrass him. Since she had no opportunity to caution the children, she proceeded as carefully as possible.

As the class time came to a close, she began to relax and asked the children to join her in their usual closing ceremony. "Let's make our churches," she said. "Here's the church and there's the steeple. Open the door and there's—" The awful consequence of her action struck her. She had done the very thing she had feared the children would do. As she stood there speechless, the little girl sitting next to the boy reached over and placed her left hand in his right hand and said, "Davey, let's make this church together."

Each of us as believers is part of the Church. Jesus said, "I will build my church; and the gates of hell shall not prevail against it" (Matthew 16:18). The church of Jesus Christ is unique in its nature and its purpose. The purpose of the Church is to proclaim the lordship of Jesus Christ in our world.

Many organizations contribute to the quality of life. As an active member and past president of the Downtown Kiwanis Club of Athens, I was involved in helping our community in many ways. We rang bells for the Salvation Army at Christ-mastime and sold popcorn for the Youth Soccer League. We ushered at community religious services and did many other things to help our community.

Many civic groups contribute to community life, but none of them compares to the Church. Why? Because Jesus offers hope to the world through His church. He is its Head, building it as He sees fit. He has promised absolute victory to the Church when He returns. No other organization has that kind of prom-ise.

I praise the Lord that I am part of His church. I paid dues to belong to the Kiwanis club, but Jesus paid the price for me to belong to the Church. He purchased and sealed my redemp-tion with His blood on the cross. Although I had many close friends in the Kiwanis club, those who were also a part of the Lord's church were much more than friends. They are my broth-ers and sisters. I thank God daily that I am privileged to belong to His church.

The Greek word for "church" is *ekklesia*. It is used at least 115 times in the New Testament and literally means the "called-out ones." The Church is the "whole company of the redeemed." All born-again persons are members of the Church. We have been called out of the world system, the kingdom of darkness, into the kingdom of light.

What is the true nature of the Church? Paul addresses this question in the Book of Ephesians. He emphatically declares that the Church is (1) the bride of Christ, (2) the building of God, and (3) the body of Christ. In this chapter, we will look more closely at the Church as the body of Christ.

In Ephesians 1:22 and 23, Paul says, "God placed all things under his feet and appointed him to be head over everything for the church, which is his body, the fullness of him who fills everything in every way" (NIV). Inspired by the Holy Spirit, Paul makes it plain: The Church is Christ's body, and Jesus is the Head.

The analogy of the Church as the body of Christ is a very important one. If we are to understand how God wants us to minister to the world and to each other, we must fully understand the nature of the Church as His body. If we are to live in vital relationship with one another and accomplish our God-given mandate, then we must recognize our individual functions within His body.

Paul, in 1 Corinthians 12:12-27, gives us greater insight into the body of Christ. Three times in this passage he emphasizes that the Church is one body composed of many members (vv. 12,14,20). Every born-again believer, as a member of the body of Christ, is an integral and necessary part of God's plan and purpose in the world.

Paul also offers the following basic principles about the body of Christ, the Church.

No Unessential Members

The first principle is that all the members of the Church are necessary. There are no unimportant or inferior members. "If the foot shall say, Because I am not the hand, I am not of the body; is it therefore not of the body?" (v. 15). Many Christians do not minister for the Lord because they feel unneeded or inferior. They may have grown up in families where it was implied that they were not important. Some may even have been told they were not wanted.

Our self-concept influences our relationships in the body of Christ. It also affects our ministry. Let us constantly remind ourselves that we are God's children. We are important to Him, and He loves us just as we are. We don't have to do anything to gain His love and favor. Even though He may not approve of everything we do, He still thinks we are the greatest. He is proud of us. "Both the one who makes men holy and those who are made holy are of the same family. So Jesus is not ashamed to call them brothers" (Hebrews 2:11, NIV).

When God looked at the man and woman He had created, He said, "Very good." No part of our human body is inferior or unnecessary. Neither is any part of Christ's body, the Church. When God saved you, He placed you as a vital member of His body. You may not be a prominent member. You may be a supporting joint or ligament. But that is a very important role. You and your ministry are essential for the proper functioning of the body of Christ. Believe that!

Sometimes I have felt inferior when comparing myself with other pastors. Amid all the great fellowship, preaching, and inspiration at sectional, district, and General Council gatherings, sometimes I have felt, *I don't belong here.* I have come home from a few of those meetings very heavyhearted, because I had fallen into the trap of comparing my church with someone else's. I judged my preaching against that of the Council speaker and came up short in my own eyes. I felt inferior, miserable, second-rate, and unimportant. I believed something was wrong with me, and I did not consider myself very useful to the Kingdom.

I am not the only one who has had these feelings. This is exactly the trap into which the enemy of our soul wants us to fall. He often succeeds in causing us to measure ourselves with others. Yet Paul said it was not wise to compare ourselves among ourselves.

Our effectiveness for the Lord is minimized, if not paralyzed, when we compare ourselves with others. By doing this, one of two results is assured. Either we will appear to be better and fall victim to pride, or we will judge ourselves to be worse and wallow in inferiority. Paul knew this: "What stupidity! . . . Our goal is to measure up to God's plan for us" (2 Corinthians 10:12,13, *The Living Bible*).

Stop comparing yourself with others, and see yourself as God does. Look in the mirror and see a beloved child. You are not inferior; you are necessary to the Lord. Paul further writes, "Nay, much more those members of the body, which seem to be more feeble, are necessary [indispensable]" (1 Corinthians 12:22). The key word here is "seem." In our human estimation, some parts seem feeble and weak. But in God's estimation (what really counts), every member of the body of Christ is absolutely necessary.

Diversity of Members

The second major principle in 1 Corinthians 12 is that of diversity within the Church: "If the whole body were an eye, where were the hearing? If the whole were hearing, where were the smelling?" (12:17). It is good that we are different from each other in some ways. I am glad my body is not made up of 139 arms and 97 legs. I am equally happy that the local church I pastor is not made up of all preachers. There is not room for too many members having identical ministries in any one church. Imagine the confusion on Sunday morning in your church if everyone were a Sunday school superintendent. Or even worse, what if everyone wanted to direct the choir?

One of the beauties of the human body is its diversity. Likewise, one of the beauties of the Church is its diversity. We are all different, and that is the way it is supposed to be. A proper understanding of our diversity will help minimize the competition among us.

Since birth, we have been competing. We compete in our families for attention and love. We compete in elementary school for social acceptance. We compete in high school for good grades or a place on the football team or cheerleading squad. In college we compete for "that cute coed" or "that handsome guy." After college, we compete for jobs.

Competition in its place is an acceptable motivator. Unfortunately, this spirit of competition has elbowed its way into the Church.   How often have our churches competed against each other for the ministry of a well-known speaker or musician so we could fill our auditorium on Sunday night? How often have we competed for the ministry of a talented youth pastor, wooing him away from his place of ministry with promises of a better salary and benefits package? How often have we competed against each other to draw into *our* fellowship the new Christian family that just moved into town?

I will never forget my first week at Bible college. I was bombarded with seven or eight invitations to attend and become part of the community's local churches. I felt very flattered to be courted by so many churches. Yet I wonder what would have happened if that same energy had been used to reach the unsaved in that community.

I am not discouraging aggressiveness in reaching out into our communities, but I am throwing up a caution flag. Let us be careful to guard against the spirit of competition among the churches in our communities or in our constituency.

This same destructive spirit of competition even finds its way into individual members of the local church. Jealousy and anger result when we don't understand that we are different because God made us that way. We don't need to compete for God's attention or favor, because He has gifted all of us differently. If we can learn to rejoice in the beauty of our God-given diversity, this will help us guard against the deadly spirit of competition.

Unity of the Members

Third, there is unity in the Church. "Now are they many members, yet . . . one body" (1 Corinthians 12:20). "How good and pleasant it is when brothers live together in unity!" (Psalm 133:1, NIV).   Even though we have different gifts and potentials in the work of the Lord, we still must be in unity.

Paul's admonition to try "to keep the unity of the Spirit in the bond of peace" (Ephesians 4:3) is a clear recognition of the existence of friction among Christians. The Church is a diversified unity. We are different, yet one. We don't need to ask the Lord to *make* us one. He already did that at the cross. Rather, we need to pray, "Lord, *keep* us one."

We spoke earlier of the destructive force of comparison and competition. Let us now consider *cooperation*. We are many members, but only *one* body. The key to effective ministry in our churches is cooperation and encouragement. The relationship between diversity, unity, cooperation, and encouragement is clearly illustrated by an incident in the life of Moses.

When Moses was instructing the Israelites just before their entry into the Promised Land, he recounted to them the words the Lord had spoken to him:

> Get thee up into the top of Pisgah, and lift up thine eyes
> westward, and northward, and southward, and eastward,
> and behold it with thine eyes: for thou shalt not go over
> this Jordan. But charge Joshua, and encourage him, and
> strengthen him: for . . . he shall cause them to inherit the
> land which thou shalt see (Deuteronomy 3:27,28).

What a tall order! God had used Moses to bring Israel to the edge of Canaan, and now they were ready to enter. But because of Moses' disobedience, he was not allowed to enter the Promised Land or to lead the people any farther. So God said, "Encourage Joshua." In essence He was saying, "I am relieving you of leadership responsibility over the Children of Israel, but I want you to support, encourage, and strengthen the man who is replacing you."

It is one thing to resign and support your successor. It is a far different thing to be fired, and then wholeheartedly encourage and strengthen your replacement. The two men of God, Moses and Joshua, had different responsibilities. Moses' responsibility was to bring Israel to the edge of Canaan. Joshua's was to lead them into battle to conquer and subdue the inhabitants of the land. At the same time, each was to support the other, and unity was to prevail. The greatness of Moses shone through again; he was obedient to a very difficult command. He did encourage Joshua. Moses was successful in this his last assignment.

This is the kind of relationship we must strive for in our churches. Though we are diverse, with different gifts, talents, and functions, God still longs for us to be one in Him, united in the Spirit of Christ. His prayer must be answered: "That they all may be one: as thou, Father, art in me, and I in thee, that they also may be one in us: that the world may believe that thou hast sent me" (John 17:21). The unity of our members will convince the world of the validity of our message!

Members Need Each Other

Paul's fourth principle in 1 Corinthians 12 is that as members of the Church we need each other. There is no room for self-sufficiency or superiority. "The eye cannot say unto the hand, I have no need of thee: nor again the head to the feet, I have no need of you" (1 Corinthians 12:21). Verse 21 shows the other side of the coin seen in verses 16 and 17. The earlier verses speak of inferiority, verse 21 speaks of superiority.

The church of Jesus Christ cannot tolerate the spirit of pride. Verse 21 is the great leveler. No one in Christ's church is more important than anyone else. God neither has nor needs superstars. True, some are more in the forefront than others, and some gain more publicity and acclaim than others. That is to be expected. In the natural, when we comment on how beautiful or handsome a person is, we generally are speaking of attractive facial features. Yet is your face more important than your liver? Absolutely not!

We must never say of someone, "I don't need you." Great care must be taken to assure that as we grow as a fellowship or as local churches, we don't fall prey to the temptation of classifying Christians socially, economically, educationally, and spiritually. Every church needs all kinds of members. We cannot treat the rich better than the poor and expect to be blessed by God. Our goal should be to help each person become part of our church.

The pastor needs everyone in the congregation, just as everyone in the congregation needs the pastor. The Sunday school teacher needs each member of his class, and each student needs the teacher. We are *all* members of His body, His flesh, His bones. The destructive spirit of pride and superiority must be dealt with in our lives. The pastor is no better than the members of the church, and they are no better than he is. Every Christian fuctions differently. You exercise your spiritual gifts. I exercise mine. We need each other.

By comparing the Church to the human body, we have observed some important facts about the nature of the Church. Now we will examine how the local church often functions, both negatively and positively. Allow me to first address the functions of the church from the negative side.

No Dictators Need Apply

Frst, the church should not function as a pastoral dictatorship. I was so relieved when I finally realized I was not in charge of the Lord's church. In fact, I'm not even in charge of the local church I pastor. I am an undershepherd, a colaborer with the Chief Shepherd, placed there to help guide, love, teach, and train God's people.

Several reminders for pastors are in order here. "The servant of the Lord must not strive; but be gentle unto all men" (2 Timothy 2:24). God's shepherds are gentle shepherds. Firmness is in order from time to time, but harshness is never allowed. Another reminder:

> Be shepherds of God's flock that is under your care, serving as overseers—not because you must, but because you are willing, as God wants you to be; not greedy for money, but eager to serve; not lording it over those entrusted to you, but being examples to the flock (1 Peter 5:2,3, NIV).

A dictator lords it over others. He strives and is certainly not gentle. God's servant in the leadership of the local church is not to be dictatorial in any way. There is an art to being firmly gentle. It takes wisdom to have the oversight of people and yet not be overbearing. Jesus is the perfect example. The disciples recognized Him as their Lord and Master (John 13:13)—which was correct. Yet He reminded them, "I am among you as one who serves" (Luke 22:27, NIV).

The pastor should never be a dictator. I have often told my Equipping for Ministry Sunday School Class, "I will not, nor can I, nor would I want to tell you how you must serve God, or in what capacity." Christ, and He alone, is the Lord of the Church.

Destructive Power Struggles

Just as the church should not function as a pastoral dictatorship, it must also not be a deacon board rulership. Remember that a deacon is a servant. Many churches are ineffective because of a constant struggle between the pastor and the lay leadership. This power struggle often is born out of a spirit of competition. How much more beautiful it is when the pastor understands his place in the Body and does not "lord it over God's heritage," and the deacon board and other lay leaders do not try to control the church.

I thank God that the men who have served on our Board of Ministry and as ministering elders have understood their place in the church. Theirs is neither a subordinate place nor a demeaning one. Together we form a team.

Once as I was watching my favorite college football team intensely struggling to win the game, I noticed how they huddled after each play. Standing in a circle, they held hands while the quarterback called the next play. Here were 11 grown men, all but one exceeding 200 pounds, holding hands before 80,000 fans and a national TV audience. They were one. The quarterback was the recognized leader, yet they all contributed. And they won! What a picture of leadership for our local churches: holding hands together, encouraging each other, supporting each other, fighting for, not against, each other.

Gifted, Therefore Chosen

The church should not function as a democracy. A study of the selection of seven deacons in Acts 6:1-7 reveals that they were chosen on the basis of their spiritual gifts and their commitment to Christ and the local church. Although the democratic process is sometimes necessary, it often complicates getting people God has gifted for the task. While I pastored New Life Assembly, the Sunday school superintendent was appointed on the basis of her recognized gifts of administration and leadership. She was committed to the Sunday school and felt a strong burden to minister in that capacity.

The church should function just as the body does. Christ, the Head, gives direction and oversight. From Him, the body is joined together perfectly and grows together in the Spirit. Leadership is chosen as the Holy Spirit gives direction through fasting and prayer.

Remember that Paul and Barnabas were *not elected* to be the first missionaries in the Early Church. "As they ministered to the Lord, and fasted, the Holy Ghost said, Separate me Barnabas and Saul for the work whereunto *I* have called them" (Acts 13:2). They were *selected* as the Holy Spirit confirmed His call on their lives to the church.

When the body functions with each member contributing to its growth, much less friction and opposition occurs in the church. Each person understands his role. There is less competition, and cooperation prevails. The pastor understands his position as the God-placed shepherd in the flock, training and equipping the saints for the work of the ministry. The congregation understands this, too, and gives the pastor the liberty to minister and lead. He is not threatened by strong lay leaders, because they understand their role. What a beautiful arrangement. We believe in the power of the Holy Spirit to lead and guide an individual's life. We must also believe in the power of the Spirit to guide and lead the local church.

Does that sound like an ideal? Can it really happen? Can a church grow together into the stature of Jesus Christ and present a powerfully consistent witness to a watching community? Yes! It is happening in congregations that understand the true nature of the Church, congregations that recognize that

> All the members of the church are necessary;
> There is diversity in the church;
> There is unity in the church; and
> We need each other in the church.

Churches that function Biblically in the spirit of love will stand strong and tall. Without undue comparison or competition, they allow Christ, the Head, to guide and direct through faithful leadership.

3

Ministry—Everyone's Responsibility

Christianity has never been, is not now, and never will be a spectator sport. The beautiful truth of the Word is that every Christian is a minister. Yes, *you* are a minister of the Lord Jesus Christ.

In too many churches today, the pastor and the other "professional clergy" are seen as The Ministers. They are expected to carry out "the ministry of the church." They take care of the visitation, counseling, preaching, organizing, driving the young people to a retreat, planning the music, etc. What happens as a result? They wear themselves out, burn themselves out, and become largely ineffective. The pastor's family also suffers as a result of the stress the pastor feels. Meanwhile, on the sidelines wait scores of people who need to experience the joy of serving the Lord. Not only do they need to serve, they *want* to serve. They are saying, "Give me an opportunity. Just show me how."

Yes, the pastor, evangelist, and missionary are ministers, but we do an injustice to the term *minister* by limiting it to those offices and individuals. Since pastors are constantly referred to as "our minister," church members get the feeling that only pastors are ministers of the Lord. The word has taken on a much narrower meaning than the Scriptures ever intended. Far too many are sitting on the sidelines in our churches.

Spectators or Ministers

I used to think the person in the pew was spiritually complacent or even lazy, but I've changed my viewpoint. I now believe the vast majority of Christians want to serve Christ to the best of their abilities. They are eagerly awaiting an opportunity. Many, sitting on the edge of the pew, are saying, "Teach us! Help us!"

The potential in the church of Jesus Christ excites me. God has been pouring out His Holy Spirit, and the average membership of our churches is increasing faster than at any other time in our history. But are we reaching our world? Are we growing in the right way? The only way to reach our world for Jesus Christ is to mobilize every Christian to minister by exercising his God-given gifts.

You may say, "I'm just a layperson. What can I do?" First, stop saying, "I'm just a layperson." Instead, say, "I am a minister of Christ. I am His servant, the salt of the earth, the light of the world." (See Matthew 5:13,14.) Your coworkers don't care whether you are ordained or not. Your neighbor reaching out for love in the midst of a crisis doesn't ask to see a ministerial license. The little lady in the nursing home or the elderly man in the hospital needs a loving, caring, Christ-sent servant of the Lord to take his hand and pray with him.

What is ministry anyway? It is service rendered in the name of the Lord, supplying someone else's needs. The New Testament word for "ministry" is *diakonia*. The "minister" is the *diakonos*, and "to minister" is *diakoneō*. Jesus used these words as He said to His disciples, "Whosoever will be great among you, let him be your minister [*diakonos*]. . . . Even as the Son of man came not to be ministered unto [*diakoneō*], but to minister [*diakoneō*], and to give his life a ransom for many" (Matthew 20:26,28).

Jesus—The Source

From the Biblical perspective, there are at least five important concepts regarding ministry.

First, the source of ministry is Jesus. In Acts 20:24 Paul told the Ephesian elders that he intended to finish both his course and his ministry. Paul's ministry was to testify of the good news of the grace of God. The Lord Jesus gave him this ministry, and it was Jesus who directed him in the fulfillment of his ministry. (See Acts 26:15-18.)

The local church, pastor, or deacon board cannot give any Christian a ministry. While God may use them to help Christians find their ministry, only Jesus gives the ministry. He alone is the Source. "In him we live, and move, and have our being" (Acts 17:28; see also John 3:27; 15:5). In spite of our former sins, present weaknesses, and future failures, He still calls us to minister. Without bragging or boasting, we can say, "I am a minister of the Lord Jesus Christ."

Each church has one pastor; some churches have several assistant pastors. But each local church has many ministers. Some of these ministers aren't as active as they should be; some are on a self-proclaimed leave of absence. But all the born-again Christians in the church are its ministers. God has given a ministry to each of them (See 1 Corinthians 12:28).

Jesus—The Example

A second principle is that our example of ministry is also Jesus. Mark 10:45 reads, "The Son of man came not to be ministered unto, but to minister." Jesus spent 33 years on the earth; He didn't just come to die. He spent 3 full years in public ministry, showing us how to minister. He is our example of the proper attitude in ministry.

Christ spent himself on others. He unselfishly poured His entire life into His followers and the world. He could have come for others to serve Him, but He didn't. No! He came to serve. His servant example was epitomized at the Last Supper. He took the servant's towel, wrapped it around his waist, and washed the disciples' feet. Only a servant was expected to do this.

Whether He was healing a leper or holding a child, casting out a demon or having dinner with sinners, Jesus was a servant. When He was teaching the multitudes, He was a servant.

He came to minister, and He was the perfect example of servanthood. Let us always see Jesus, the humble servant, as the perfect example of ministry. In Paul's words, "The attitude you should have is the one that Christ Jesus has: He . . . took the nature of a servant" (Philippians 2:5, Today's English Version).

Varieties of Ministry

Third, many varieties of ministry are available. Paul clearly stated in 1 Corinthians 12:5, "There are different ways of serving [*diakonia*], but the same Lord is served" (TEV). This fact is illustrated in various New Testament examples.

In Mark 1:31, Jesus healed Peter's mother-in-law, and she rose immediately and "ministered" to them. Did she preach or teach? No, her ministry at the time was as a hostess. Using the gift of hospitality, she served Jesus and His disciples by feeding them and helping them to relax, thus preparing them to continue their ministry. In the midst of their arduous schedule of ministry, a woman grateful for her healing ministered to Christ. Likewise, in Luke 10:40, we are reminded of Martha's service (ministry) as a cook, preparing a meal in her home for Christ and His disciples.

Another example of ministry is seen in Acts 6:4. The apostles ministered by studying, teaching, and preaching the Word of God. Just as Martha had prepared and served food for people's physical needs, the apostles prepared and served food for people's spiritual needs.

Still another kind of ministry is seen in 1 Timothy 3:10: "Then let them use the office of a deacon. . . ." "Deacon" is used for the same Greek word (*diakonos*) translated "minister." New Testament deacons were servants.

By taking part in the founding of New Life Assembly of Athens, I had the privilege and responsibility of helping to shape its philosophy of leadership. We tried to be consistent in the titles we gave the church leadership. Our deacon board was called the board of ministry. Each of the five members was truly a servant. Another group of men in the church was known as the "ministering elders." These spiritually mature and scripturally qualified men ministered with the pastor in visitation, new Christian follow-up, and other needed tasks. They did not view themselves as rulers, but rather as servants. Together, we served the church as Biblical deacons and elders.

Finally, in Acts 11:29, the Christians at Antioch ministered by sending relief (that is, offerings) to the Judean Christians who were in the midst of a famine. Also, in 2 Corinthians 8:4; 9:1,12, the word *diakonos* is used by Paul to refer to "giving money."

Ministry, then, is much more than pastoring and evangelizing or being a missionary on a foreign field. Ministry is service done in the name of the Lord. For most Christians, ministry takes place only several hours during the week inside the church building. But ministry is not limited to what is done inside the church building. The healthy church sees more ministry done outside the walls of the church than inside. A committed servant-Christian will minister in many ways throughout the week wherever he or she is.

Total Participation

A fourth principle regarding ministry is that participation is for everyone. In Ephesians 4:11,12, Paul clearly states how the work of the Lord is to be done. God has given as gifts to the church apostles, prophets, evangelists, and pastor-teachers. These four have one primary function: "to prepare God's people for works of service" (NIV). The word used in verse 12 for "prepare" ("perfecting" in the KJV) is the Greek word *katartismos*. It means "a fitting or preparing fully."

The church is to be a training ground. The pastor and other leaders are to be the faculty, preparing and outfitting the members for their own ministries. This is exactly what Paul meant in Ephesians 4:12. All the believers in Ephesus were to "do the work of the ministry." Today, participation in ministry is still for everyone.

Peter also emphasizes this in his epistle, calling for 100-

percent participation in ministry by the saints. "*Each one* [italics mine] should use whatever gift he has received to serve others, faithfully administering God's grace in its various forms" (1 Peter 4:10, NIV).

The notion of "that's what we are paying the pastor for" must be discarded. Each child of God is a minister, required by the Lord to be an active participant. What would happen if everyone in your church would say, "Lord, I am Your servant. I will participate in the ministry of the church"? The possibilities are staggering. The local church, and the Church worldwide, would be edified and strengthened. This alone should be reason enough to pursue this course of action.

Ministry—Everyone's Responsibility

The fifth principle is that everyone has the responsibility to minister. We have already noted that there are varieties of ministry and that everyone has the privilege of participating in ministry. The Scriptures also clearly state that each Christian has a responsibility to fulfill the ministry to which the Lord has called him.

First Corinthians 16:15 reads, "Ye know the house of Stephanas, . . . the firstfruits of Achaia, and that they have addicted themselves to the ministry of the saints." The members of Stephanas' household were among the first converts under Paul's ministry in Corinth (1 Corinthians 1:16). However, they did not stop with conversion or water baptism. They continued to grow in the faith and in their commitment to Jesus Christ. In this closing comment of 1 Corinthians, Paul mentions that Stephanas' family *addicted* themselves to the ministry. Ministry was a strong commitment, a passion, a priority. Just as the drug addict must have his drugs or he suffers withdrawal, this family *had* to minister for the Lord or they weren't happy. They had a passion to fulfill their calling in the Lord.

The other challenging Scripture verse is 2 Timothy 4:5. Here Paul, shortly before his death, gives last-minute instructions to his spiritual son Timothy. Paul tells him, "Discharge all the duties of your ministry" (NIV). This command is not for pastors and evangelists only. It is for each Christian.

God is bringing into His church all of the people needed to reach the world. He has placed them as Sunday school teachers, Royal Rangers leaders, greeters, ushers, encouragers, hospital visitors, intercessors, pastors, custodians, secretaries, district superintendents, youth workers, writers, and on and on. Once they are placed by God, He asks each one to fulfill his ministry. You have that responsibility.

What has God called you to do? If you know, then do it. Fulfill your ministry. If you do not know what God wants you to do, now is the time to begin to find out. Submit yourself to the Holy Spirit and be open to His leading, and you will discover God's will for you.

Ministry in the Workplace

In his book *Partners in Ministry*, James Garlow refers to "churchly ministry" and "vocational ministry." While we don't want to compartmentalize our ministry, neither do we want to ignore these two areas of ministry. The way a person spends 40 or more hours each week is extremely important to the Lord and His church. God has called you to minister in your workplace.

Most people who come to Christ and join our churches come at the invitation and urging of a close friend or relative. Often these friendships are cultivated at work. For example, one of our ministering elders at New Life Assembly, John, saw his occupation of coal miner as a ministry. His life was well received because he worked hard, did his best, and lived a consistent Christian life before his fellow workers. During our weekly Tuesday morning prayer meetings, we would often pray for some of his coworkers who needed Christ. How thrilling it was the day John led one of these men to Christ at our church altar. He saw his workplace as part of his ministry to the Lord. As a result, several have now received Christ as Saviour.

Ministry in Christ's Church

Important ministries do take place each Sunday when God's people come together. Musicians are God's ministers to encourage and strengthen us. Bible teachers and nursery attendants minister to us and our children.

God wants us to do well in both spheres of ministry. He is pleased when we do our best in our vocational ministry. He is also honored when we do our best in the ministry He has given us in the local church. It is not an either/or situation; God expects ministry in both areas.

Many Christians face a predicament. They want to minister for the Lord, but they see their secular employment as a hindrance rather than a tool for effective ministry. Because of this, they say to their pastor, "I want to be involved in full-time ministry." My reply is, "You already are."

Our terminology has contributed to this problem. Both pastors and other Christian leaders often refer to their ministry as "full-time." Does that mean the members of our congregation are involved in "part-time" or "half-time" ministry? Absolutely not! Each child of God who is walking in communion with the Lord is in full-time ministry. We are *all* servants *all* of the time.

The church cannot afford to allow a few to do all the work while the majority watch. Every Christian has a ministry:

The *source* of his ministry is Jesus.

The *example* of his ministry is Jesus.

There are many *varieties* of ministry.

Everyone is to participate in a ministry.

Everyone has a *responsibility* to fulfill a ministry.

It is the task of the church's leadership to help train its members for effective ministry. Specific steps toward accomplishing this task will be discussed in later chapters.

4

Spiritual Gifts

On a trip around the world, a man and his wife arrived in Switzerland for a 3-day stay. Weary from traveling, they checked into their hotel late in the afternoon and decided to eat in the hotel dining room. The evening meal was excellent but expensive. When they asked the waiter to add the cost to their hotel bill, he nodded, smiling in a knowing way.

To save money the couple ate most of their other meals away from the hotel, but they never had food as fine as on that first evening. Receiving their hotel bill at the end of their stay, they noticed they had not been charged for the one dinner. To their chagrin, they learned the cost of their room had included meals. They could have eaten every meal for all 3 days in the hotel dining room at no extra cost.

How like so many Christians! Unaware of what wealth the Holy Spirit has given them in the form of spiritual gifts, they go through life without using the resources available to them.

God wants His church to grow to its full potential, mature and complete. Spiritual gifts are part of God's plan to bring the Church to the highest possible level of maturity and unity. He gives spiritual gifts to enhance the vitality and growth of the Body. Furthermore, there is a direct correlation between the proper use of spiritual gifts and the effectiveness of our ministry.

What Are Spiritual Gifts?

Dr. Ken Kinghorn, seminary professor and author of *Gifts*

of the Spirit, defines a spiritual gift as "a supernatural ability or capacity given by God to enable the Christian to minister (serve)."[1] Dr. Peter Wagner offers this definition: "A special attribute given by the Holy Spirit to every member of the body according to God's grace for use in the body."[2]

In the New Testament several Greek words are translated "spiritual gift." And they occur not only in 1 Corinthians 12:8-10 but in 1 Corinthians 12:28, Ephesians 4:11, Romans 12:6-8, and 1 Peter 4:9,10 as well. The most common Greek word is *charisma*. The plural is *charismata*. The contemporary move of the Holy Spirit known as the charismatic movement is based on the revival of the importance of the Holy Spirit and His gifts within the body of Christ.

Although the word *charismata* is not the only word used in the New Testament for the term "spiritual gifts," it is the most common one. (Two other Greek words, *pneumatikos* and *dōmata*, are also used.) What does *charismata* mean? It is a gift of God's grace bestowed by the Holy Spirit on a believer. The word *grace* is important to our understanding of spiritual gifts. Spiritual gifts, like salvation, are a result of God's unmerited, undeserved favor.

Four general observations about spiritual gifts can be made. Spiritual gifts are given (1) by the Holy Spirit, (2) for service, (3) through God's grace, and (4) to every believer. To further understand spiritual gifts, let's briefly discuss what spiritual gifts are not.

Not Natural Talents

Because God created man beautifully and wonderfully, his offspring possess many natural abilities. Some possess great mental abilities, while others possess great athletic ability. Still others have natural musical ability. Everyone has natural talents—but spiritual gifts are limited to Christians. Unbelievers do not have spiritual gifts, but every Christian has one or more.

It is difficult at times to tell the difference between natural talents and spiritual gifts. The distinction is not always clear. After conversion, God will often use a natural ability or talent to edify the body of Christ. For example, a person who has the ability to organize, set goals, and plan may be given the spiritual gift of administration. However, God is not bound to work in any predetermined or expected manner. He may choose to gift that person in an altogether different area.

Not Christian Responsibilities

In our churches we have ushers, choir members, superintendents, greeters, board members, etc. The responsibilities of these positions are important. But so many things need to be done in the Lord's work that we don't always stop and examine our level of giftedness for the task at hand. We just roll up our sleeves and do it.

However, as important as these tasks are, they are not spiritual gifts.

Not Spiritual Fruit

The fruit of the Spirit has to do with the quality of our lives and our relationship with others. Spiritual gifts, on the other hand, have to do with our calling and function in ministry. The fruit is what we are (loving, joyful, peaceful, patient, gentle, faithful, humble, temperate, good, upright). The gifts are what we do.

In discussing the difference between the gifts of the Spirit and the fruit of the Spirit, a friend of mine uses an analogy. He compares the gifts of the Spirit to a railroad car and the fruit to the tracks. Just as railroad cars are effective only when riding on the tracks, so the gifts of the Spirit are effective only when the person manifesting the gifts is also manifesting the fruit. When the fruit of the Spirit ceases to grow in our lives, the gifts of the Spirit are of little value. After all, how far can a railroad car go without tracks? Spirit-given abilities are important, but they mean very little without Spirit-produced fruit.

In a day when much emphasis is being given to the gifts of

the Spirit, we must remember that God places the highest priority on character and godly behavior, on "doing what love does." Gifts without love and the other Christlike qualities are nerve-racking and bothersome, like "clanging cymbals." Love is the fruit that gives value to the gifts (1 Corinthians 13:1-3).

To understand how spiritual gifts are related to the ministry of each believer, we will discuss six principles regarding spiritual gifts.[3] Keep in mind that we are not speaking of only the nine gifts mentioned in 1 Corinthians 12:8-10, but also those mentioned in 1 Corinthians 12:28, Ephesians 4:11, Romans 12:6-8, and 1 Peter 4:9,10.

Given According to God's Grace

"But unto every one of us is given grace according to the measure of the gift of Christ" (Ephesians 4:7). Spiritual gifts are *received*, not *achieved*. This is difficult for some to understand. For years, a dedicated saint faithfully serves God. He longs for the Holy Spirit to use him in a particular way. He fasts, asks, begs, and cajoles God for a particular gift of the Spirit. Then a newly saved, Spirit-filled Christian comes along, and God uses this person in the very way the older Christian has longed to be used by the Lord. This can produce misunderstandings, resentment, and jealousy.

God makes it clear why this happens. The gifts cannot be earned by good behavior. We are not on a time schedule to receive "spiritual merit raises" every few years. God gives the gifts according to His grace.

Given According to God's Wisdom

"All these are the work of one and the same Spirit, and He gives them to each one, just as He determines" (1 Corinthians 12:11, NIV). For a number of years, especially while a Bible college student and a rookie pastor, I would pray for specific spiritual gifts. For several months I would pray for the gift of the word of wisdom, then for the discerning of spirits. (Oddly enough, I never found myself praying for the gift of serving, or helps, or mercy.) I finally realized that Scripture does not encourage us to pray for specific spiritual gifts. The Bible does encourage us to "covet earnestly the best gifts" (1 Corinthians 12:31).

What is the best gift? Is it prophecy, faith, or the working of miracles? *The best gift is the one most needed at the time.* For example, if I'm walking down the street and come upon a man lying on the ground in excruciating pain, the gift of tongues isn't needed. I need the gift of healing. Or, if we need to organize a work party at the church to construct a new platform, we don't need the gift of prophecy. We need the gift of administration to help plan and organize, the gift of leadership to motivate and inspire the men to work diligently, and the gift of helps in men who know how to build a platform that will look nice and meet our need (see Exodus 35:30,31). The best gift, then, is the one most needed at a particular time.

Some time ago I heard a dynamic sermon preached from Judges 6 by Rev. Hardy Steinberg at the Ohio Family Camp. The Children of Israel were in bondage to the Midianites. After 7 years of oppression, the Israelites called out to the Lord, and God found Gideon to deliver them. Gideon was hiding behind the barn, hoping the enemy would not see him. The angel of the Lord came to Gideon and announced, "The Lord is with thee, thou mighty man of valour." Gideon's response was, "How can I save Israel? My clan is the weakest in Manasseh, and I am the least in my family" (Judges 6:15, NIV).

Gideon felt inferior and incapable of the assigned task. "How could God possibly use me?" God knew his weaknesses and insufficiencies. Yet He called him, and Gideon obeyed. Then the Spirit of the Lord came upon Gideon (6:34). Brother Steinberg shared the literal meaning of that sentence: *"But the Spirit of the Lord clothed himself with Gideon."*

How was Gideon to lead Israel against these formidable enemies? "The Spirit of the Lord clothed himself with Gideon." It was as if the Holy Spirit said, "I need a body to put on like a man puts on a suit of clothes so I can defeat the enemy and

Israel can be free again." Gideon did not need a large army because, in reality, the Holy Spirit was leading the charge. Gideon was the human body the Holy Spirit was wearing at the time.

Nearly every day I pray, "Lord, fill me with Your Spirit for this day. And, Lord, I am available for the Holy Spirit to use in whatever work needs to be done today." If I meet a sick child, I want the Holy Spirit to clothe himself with me, bringing healing to him. If I meet a discouraged brother, I want the Holy Spirit to clothe himself with me so we can encourage him. I desire to be so filled with the Holy Spirit, and so yielded to the Lord's will, that He can manifest His Spirit through me in healing, prophecy, mercy, or whatever gift He chooses.

Every Christian Can Exercise Spiritual Gifts

"The manifestation of the Spirit is given to *every man* to profit withal" (1 Corinthians 12:7; see also 1 Peter 4:10). Spiritual gifts are not the property of the clergy. They are not for some elite group of Christians. Rather, God intends that every Christian, full of the Holy Spirit, be used by Him to edify the Church through spiritual gifts. There are no rich or poor, big or little, in God's kingdom. My former district superintendent, Rev. Arthur Parsons, often said, "There are big churches and little churches. But there are no big preachers and no little preachers."

Gifts Are To Glorify God

Each one should use whatever gift he has received to serve others, faithfully administering God's grace in its various forms. If anyone speaks, he should do it as one speaking the very words of God. If anyone serves, he should do it with the strength God provides, so that in all things God may be praised through Jesus Christ. To Him be the glory and the power for ever and ever. Amen (1 Peter 4:10,11, NIV).

Clearly, spiritual gifts are not given for the purpose of our own advancement or glory. They are given to help us minister more effectively. God gives the gift of giving, not so the giver can be glorified, but that God may be glorified as the need is met.

Why do we serve? Why do we preach? Why do we sing? Is it for the glory of God? Let us pray "that God in all things may be glorified through Jesus Christ, to whom be praise and dominion forever and ever!"

Gifts Are Needed by the Church

Jesus commanded, "Stay in the city until you have been clothed with power from on high" (Luke 24:49, NIV). Too many Christians in too many churches have resorted to human talent and ingenuity to do the work of the Lord. They labor sincerely, but there is no lasting fruit. Jesus said,

> Abide in me, and I in you: As the branch cannot bear fruit of itself, except it abide in the vine; no more can ye, except ye abide in me. I am the vine, ye are the branches. He that abideth in me, and I in him, the same bringeth forth much fruit; for without me ye can do nothing (John 15:4,5).

We will be effective as the Holy Spirit is actively involved in our lives, filling, enabling, and directing us. How thankful we are for our human talents; they have their place. But sad would be the day if they were our only resource to "go into all the world and preach the gospel." How pitiful our efforts if we were to teach, sing, preach, or evangelize in our human talents and abilities alone.

Why was the Early Church effective? People could tell they had been with Jesus. Can we settle for less? Never! Our church was born in the fire of the Holy Spirit's outpouring. With all our gadgets, computers, sound systems, and well-trained musicians, let us seek the dynamic power of the Holy Spirit as never before. Only then will the full ministry of the Church be accomplished.

Gifts Are To Accomplish God's Will

> Therefore, I urge you, brothers, in view of God's mercy,
> to offer your bodies as living sacrifices, holy and pleasing
> to God—which is your spiritual worship. Do not conform
> any longer to the pattern of this world, but be transformed
> by the renewing of your mind. Then you will be able to
> test and approve what God's will is—His good, pleasing
> and perfect will (Romans 12:1,2, NIV).

To know the will of God, we must carefully follow the instructions of the next few verses. If we are to know God's will,
we must "think soberly," not thinking of ourselves more highly
than we ought (12:3). Then, remember that we are all part of
one body in Christ, individual members with differing gifts
(12:4-6). When we begin to discern which gifts have been entrusted to us by the Holy Spirit, we will begin to understand
what God's will for our lives is. Our ministry will flow out of
the gifts He has given us.

Growing churches understand the dynamic of spiritual gifts
and have learned to maximize their effectiveness. As the Holy
Spirit is given free rein to minister through every believer, the
church grows.

---

[1]Kenneth C. Kinghorn, *Gifts of the Spirit* (Nashville, TN: Abingdon Press,
1976), p. 22.

[2]C. Peter Wagner, *Your Spiritual Gifts Can Make Your Church Grow* (Glen-
dale, CA: Gospel Light Regal Publications, 1979), p. 42.

[3]Portions of this section were adapted from Kinghorn, *Gifts of the Spirit*.

5

Gifts of the Spirit

God wants every church to grow. When Christ said, "I will build my church" (Matthew 16:18), He committed himself and all of the resources of the Godhead to the establishment and growth of His church. Among these divine resources, two major categories stand out as essential: (1) the supernatural gifts of the Spirit, the *charismata* of 1 Corinthians 12:8-10, and (2) the various ministries and offices listed in Ephesians 4:8-11 and Romans 12:6-8.

This chapter and the one following will examine each of these gifts and ministries found in the church. In both chapters, the primary emphasis will be on how these gifts and ministries can and should be operating within the congregation, not only among the staff ministers of the church. In dealing with each of these gifts and ministries, a brief definition will be given. Also, the Scripture reference where the gift/ministry is named or described will be given, as well as a Biblical example of its operation. The supernatural gifts of the Holy Spirit will be discussed in this chapter.

The nine "gifts of the Spirit" are listed in 1 Corinthians 12:8-10. Paul calls them "manifestations" in 1 Corinthians 12:7: "Now to each one the manifestation of the Spirit is given for the common good" (NIV). The word "manifestation" literally means "an uncovering, a clear display, a shining forth." This means that when these nine gifts are in operation, the Holy Spirit is revealing, or uncovering, a different aspect of His nature and work to the Church. In essence, the Holy Spirit is saying, "I am going to pull back the curtain that veils My glory and nature and reveal a part of myself to you, My children."

Donald Gee, in his book *Concerning Spiritual Gifts*, gives some insight into the purpose and function of these gifts:

> They [these spiritual gifts] were to provide a spiritual capability far mightier than the finest natural abilities could ever supply; and, deeper still, they were to provide the supernatural basis for a supernatural order of ministry. . . .
>
> There is also a purpose in the steady exercise of the gifts of the Spirit in the church far deeper than simply providing her needs on the lines of ministry. Arising from the fact that they are supernatural and divine in their origin comes this other fact—that they are a continual "manifestation of the Spirit," an abiding and inspiring reminder of His presence and power.[1]

These nine manifestations, or gifts, of the Holy Spirit are often divided into three categories, each containing three individual gifts. In other words, three gifts showing the Holy Spirit's knowledge, three showing His power, and another three showing His message.

The Manifestation of the Spirit's Knowledge

1. *The Word of Wisdom.* The first gift in this category is the word of wisdom (1 Corinthians 12:8). It has been described as the revelation of supernatural wisdom in a situation where man cannot see which way to go or which solution to choose for a given problem. When the word of wisdom is operating through an individual, it is usually clear that this wisdom is from God, not from that person himself.

An illustration of this gift is found in Acts 6:1-6. When a dispute arose between the Hebrew and Greek widows in the Early Church, the Holy Spirit guided the apostles through the word of wisdom to inaugurate the first deacon board. This provided the immediate and best solution to the dispute in the church. Through the operation of this gift of the Holy Spirit, the church continued to grow and become strong.

2. *The Word of Knowledge.* The second gift manifesting the Spirit's knowledge is the word of knowledge (1 Corinthians 12:8). This gift may be defined as the immediate impression of facts or circumstances without the aid of the senses. Many times this revelation is in the area of hidden sins or attitudes that are hindering the spiritual welfare of another person, whether an unbeliever or a fellow Christian.

The word of knowledge was manifested through Peter in Acts 5:1-11. Ananias and his wife, Sapphira, attempted to deceive Peter and the church by lying about their offering. God revealed their deception to Peter, enabling him to confront them with their sin.

3. *Discerning of Spirits.* The final "knowledge" gift is that of discerning of spirits (1 Corinthians 12:10). Discerning of spirits has been defined as the supernatural ability to know the source from which supernatural power and/or utterances come. This power may be either divine or demonic, and the utterances may be from God, Satan, or man himself. When the gift of discerning of spirits is in operation, there is no confusion concerning their source. The Holy Spirit reveals the origin of this power or utterance in order to protect and/or edify the church. One point must be remembered and emphasized. This is *not* a gift of general discernment; rather, it is the gift of discerning of *spirits.*

When Paul and Silas were ministering at Philippi (Acts 16:16-18), a demon-possessed young lady followed them continually. Day after day she cried out, "These men are the servants of the most high God, which show unto us the way of salvation" (Acts 16:17). The Holy Spirit revealed to Paul that, even though the words of her message were correct, the source of the message was demonic. As a result of this discernment, not only was the girl delivered from demonic possession, but also a church was established in the city of Philippi.

The Manifestation of the Spirit's Power

1. *Faith.* Faith (1 Corinthians 12:9) is the first gift demon-

strating the power of the Holy Spirit. By definition, the gift of faith is a supernatural bestowal of faith upon the believer, enabling him to believe for something for which he otherwise could not have believed. Peter and John manifested the gift of faith when at the gate of the temple they met a man who had never walked. God's faith dropped into Peter's heart, and the man was instantly healed. In Acts 3:16, Peter attributed this healing to faith in Jesus: "His name, through faith in his name, hath made this man strong."

2. *The Working of Miracles.* The working of miracles is the second "power" gift, found in 1 Corinthians 12:10. It is a work "contrary to nature resulting from a supernatural intervention, an interruption of the system of nature as we know it."[2] One clear example of the working of miracles is seen in Acts 9:36-41, when Peter raised Dorcas from the dead. It is significant that both prayer and a removal of doubt were involved in this miracle.

3. *The Gifts of Healings.* The last of the three gifts manifesting the Holy Spirit's power is the gifts of healings (1 Corinthians 12:9,28). This is actually a group of related gifts, not a single gift, defined as the revelation of God's power to heal sickness and disease. The gifts of healings were some of the most evident manifestations of the Holy Spirit's power in the New Testament. For example, while Paul was ministering at Ephesus (Acts 19:11,12), God revealed His limitless power and healed many who were sick and oppressed.

The Manifestation of the Spirit's Message

The final three manifestations of the Holy Spirit found in 1 Corinthians 12:8-10 relate to His message. They include prophecy, speaking in "divers kinds of tongues," and the interpretation of tongues.

1. *Prophecy.* Prophecy (1 Corinthians 12:10; Romans 12:6) is the declaration of a portion of God's total message to the church through a yielded believer, given in the language of the speaker and hearers. In discussing this gift, it is important to

distinguish it from the office of the prophet (Ephesians 4:11). Both in the Ephesians passage and in 1 Corinthians 12:28, the word "prophecy" is used. In Ephesians, the emphasis is on the person whom the Lord uses. In 1 Corinthians, it is not on the person but rather on the message given. Any yielded Spirit-filled believer can be an instrument through whom the Spirit may reveal His message to the church. The gift of prophecy is not limited to those who are prophets in the church. Most of the time, the prophecy is a declaration of what God is doing, a "forth-telling," rather than a prediction, or "foretelling."

The gift of prophecy is seen in operation in Acts 27:21-25. When Paul and the other prisoners were on board the ship going to Rome, a severe storm threatened the ship and their lives. The Holy Spirit had a message of encouragement and hope, as well as of instruction for the men, and He used Paul to give it. God promised that no one who stayed on the ship would lose his life. This was a firm declaration of what God was going to do.

2. *Divers Kinds of Tongues.* Of all the gifts of the Spirit, none has been more controversial than the gift of tongues (1 Corinthians 12:10,28). This gift may be described as the declaration of a message from God to the church through a yielded believer, given in a language previously unlearned by the speaker. This message should be accompanied by an interpretation.[3]

In some settings today, as in New Testament times, this gift has been abused. Yet, even though the Corinthian church was abusing the gift of tongues and good order was lacking, Paul still encouraged the use of the gift in a worship service (1 Corinthians 14:26) as long as it was accompanied by an interpretation (14:5,27).

3. *Interpretation of Tongues.* Closely related to the gift of tongues is the gift of interpretation of tongues (1 Corinthians 12:10). It is defined as "an inspired explanation in commonly understood language of an inspired utterance in unknown tongues."[4]

It should be emphasized that this is an *interpretation* of what was said in tongues, not a literal translation. In 1 Corinthians 14:5,26-28, Paul stresses the importance of the interpretation of a message in tongues. When interpretation follows the message in tongues, the church is edified, just as it is when a prophecy is given forth.

While these nine gifts dwell in the Holy Spirit, they are manifested through yielded believers. The Holy Spirit can reveal himself through any yielded Spirit-filled Christian at any time to meet a particular need.

There is considerable discussion regarding the relative importance of these gifts. This stems in part from Paul's admonition to "covet earnestly the best gifts" (1 Corinthians 12:31). While some promote prophecy as the "best" gift, there is equal support for some of the other gifts. In the final analysis, the best gift is the one that is most needed at the time.

God has all knowledge and all power, and He wants to communicate with us. He has arranged it so that through three of these gifts, He reveals His knowledge; through another three, He reveals His power; and through the last three, He proclaims His message to the Church.

The Gifts of the Spirit in the Church Today

The growth of many churches is stunted because these nine gifts of the Holy Spirit are not in operation on a regular basis. In other churches these gifts are operating in the lives of only a few individuals, usually the leaders of the church. But the vast majority of the membership is still not involved. While such a church may grow, it will never realize its full potential. Only when a large percentage of the members of the congregation are being used in these nine gifts will that church grow as God really wishes.

We all want our church to grow. It *will*—if we give God the liberty to minister through us. At the same time, we must recognize that Satan is doing everything in his power to prevent or hinder the church's growth. This makes it all the more imperative to have the fullness of the Holy Spirit operating within the local congregation.

Satan uses various tricks to hinder the Holy Spirit's operation. His primary tactic against the Church is the lie. Some of his favorite lies in this area include: "You aren't good enough to give a message in tongues." Or, "That isn't the Holy Spirit; it's only you wanting to interpret the message." Another lie is, "God won't heal that child when you pray for him. You'll just make a fool of yourself." Many others could be listed, but these are enough to show the type of opposition the Church faces today.

This opposition can only be overcome when three things happen. First, we must recognize that only God can give the victory over Satan. Second, we must teach about the operation of the Spirit in the Church. Finally, we must trust God enough to believe that, as we sincerely give ourselves over to Him, He will not allow us to bring reproach to Him or to His church.

While it is fairly easy to recognize that we are in a spiritual battle against Satan, most of us still try to do the fighting ourselves. This in itself shows a serious lack of teaching. The need for teaching is seen even more clearly by the following questions heard in many churches:

"Who can be used in the gifts of the Holy Spirit?"

"How do I know if God wants to use *me* in the gifts of the Spirit?"

"How can I know that it is God speaking and not just me?"

"Through which gifts will God use me?"

If we are going to see the full manifestation of the Holy Spirit in our churches, we must answer these and other questions being asked by church members. This can be done in at least two ways. First, the pastor can deliver a series of sermons on the Holy Spirit, His gifts, and our responsibilities as Pentecostal Christians. Second, we can build a series of lessons into our Christian education curriculum dealing with these topics.[5]

In the final analysis, however, the best way to see the church grow through the manifestation of these gifts of the Spirit is for the members who know how to yield to the Holy Spirit to do so. As the others see how God can and does move through these members, they will become hungry for the greater things of God and be more receptive to the sermons and lessons. More importantly, they will be more receptive to the Holy Spirit.

Let's take another look at those questions listed above. Many members of Assemblies of God churches do not understand that *any* Pentecostal believer can be used by the Holy Spirit through any of the nine gifts. There is no additional requirement beyond being baptized in the Holy Spirit and then yielding to His leading.

Following up on this point, the second question asks for assurance that God really does want to use the believer through these gifts. God's greatest wish is that we grow to full maturity in Christ. For Pentecostal believers, this means that we should become sensitive to the moving of the Holy Spirit in our lives and in the body of Christ as a whole. As we do so, God can speak through us, pray through us, and edify the Church through us. Again, the key is yielding ourselves to the Holy Spirit's direction.

Many people are very skeptical the first time the Holy Spirit moves them to speak in tongues or give a prophecy. This is natural, and God does not condemn us for being afraid. The problem arises when after three, five, or even ten times, we are still afraid to yield to the Spirit's leading. At this point the question becomes, "Do I really trust God enough to let Him use me, or am I too afraid of what others will think?"

Concerns like this are purely human; every Christian faces them sometime in his Christian walk. It is a sign of spiritual maturity when a believer says, "I don't care if I do appear foolish. I know God wants to speak through me, and I am going to let Him do it!" At this point Satan tries to convince the believer that it is not really God speaking, but the person himself. Here again, the solution lies in placing our total trust in God. If we are open to Him and are living the consistent Christian life He expects of us, then He will make it clear when He wants to speak through us.

The fourth question is one many newly Spirit-baptized believers ask. There is always an interest in the more visible gifts: speaking in tongues, interpretation of tongues, prophecy, healings, etc. These are the gifts new Pentecostal believers have seen and heard about the most. However, they must be taught that the other gifts are just as important and sometimes more needed in the local church.   They must learn that God, not we, decides which gift is seen in our lives: "He gives them to each man, just as he determines" (1 Corinthians 12:11, NIV). The Spirit decides, not us.

These four questions are typical of those asked by both new and more mature Pentecostal Christians. The answers to these and other questions are needed in the local church. The stronger and more solid the teaching on the Holy Spirit, the more likely it is that the church will see the various gifts in operation in its services and in the everyday lives of its members.

Along with these nine gifts of the Holy Spirit, God has given other ministry gifts to His church. These will be discussed in considerable detail in the following chapter. When the gifts of the Holy Spirit and the ministry gifts of Christ to the Church work together, the Church will truly grow as God wishes.

---

[1]Donald Gee, *Concerning Spiritual Gifts* (Springfield, MO: Gospel Publishing House, rev. ed., 1980), pp. 26, 27.

[2]G. Raymond Carlson, *Spiritual Dynamics* (Springfield, MO: Gospel Publishing House, 1976), p. 105.

[3]For further study on the gift of tongues, see Stanley M. Horton's book *What the Bible Says About the Holy Spirit* (Springfield, MO: Gospel Publishing House, 1976).

[4]Carlson, *Spiritual Dynamics*, p. 106.

[5]A suggested 13-week study is *Spiritual Dynamics* by G. Raymond Carlson (Springfield, MO: Gospel Publishing House), order number 02-0894. A teacher's guide is also available, order number 32-0168.

6

Ministry Gifts of Christ

The growth of a church is directly related to the spiritual gifts and ministries operating in the church. We noted at the end of chapter 4 that growing churches understand this. They plan their church programs in such a way as to maximize the impact of these spiritual gifts and ministries. A truly effective church will manifest the nine gifts of the Spirit together with the ministry gifts of Christ listed in Ephesians 4 and Romans 12.

The Early Church of Acts clearly illustrates this. When the manifestation of tongues was seen and heard on the Day of Pentecost, someone asked, "What does this mean?" (Acts 2:12, NIV). Later that day, Peter's anointed sermon prompted the question, "What shall we do?" (2:37, NIV). The church grew by at least 3,000 members that very day as these manifestations of the Spirit were seen. Other spiritual gifts and ministries (such as teaching, miracles, gifts of healings) were also operative in the same time period (2:42,43). These manifestations, combined with fellowship and worship, resulted in greater growth as "the Lord added to the church daily such as should be saved" (2:47). The gifts of healings (3:6) and the word of knowledge (5:3) were also instrumental in bringing multitudes to Christ (5:14).

Many factors are necessary for consistent and solid church growth, including vision, enthusiasm, prayer, sound Bible preaching, and personal evangelism. Attempting to proclaim Christ and help people without all the spiritual gifts and ministries operating in the local church is like trying to play basketball without a hoop. No matter how much you run up and down the court, how well you make passes, how good your offense and defense, you will never score without a hoop.

Similarly, we can do all the right things, have helpful programs, sing beautiful songs, serve Communion, pray for the sick, and much more. However, if the gifts of the Spirit are not functioning fully in the church, we will never do much scoring. Likewise, if the ministry gifts Paul described in Ephesians and Romans are not seen in a local church, it will never realize its full potential as an evangelistic outpost for Christ. Even with these gifts and ministries in operation, we must caution ourselves just as Paul did the Corinthians in 1 Corinthians 12 through 14. The free flow of the gifts of the Holy Spirit in the church must be validated by the fruit of love.

In addition to the nine gifts of the Holy Spirit listed in 1 Corinthians 12:8-10, there are several specific ministries Christ has given to the Church to help it grow. These are listed in at least three places in Paul's writings: Ephesians 4, 1 Corinthians 12:28, and Romans 12. In combining these three lists, one arrives at the following list: apostle, prophet, evangelist, pastor-teacher, helps, and administrative leadership. In addition to these, Christ has placed individuals in the church who feel called to give, to encourage, to show mercy, and to serve in whatever capacity is needed.

When these ministries are compared with the nine gifts of the Holy Spirit, it becomes clear that, while the gifts are truly manifestations of the Holy Spirit, these ministries are actually individual believers whom God has called and placed in His church to minister to it. Most of these ministries can and often are carried out by nonprofessional clergy—the layman sitting in the pew every Sunday.

In this chapter, detailed descriptions and modern equivalents of the primary ministries listed by Paul in Ephesians 4 (apostle, prophet, evangelist, pastor-teacher) will be given. In addition, brief summaries will be given of the other ministries God has given to the layman.

Christ's Gifts to the Church

Christ gave apostles, prophets, evangelists, and pastor-teachers to the Church at the time of His ascension. These four ministries are necessary to enable and equip all Christians for service to the Lord. These ministries are absolutely essential for the success of the Church and should be seen in the leaders of the local church.

1. *Apostle.* In Ephesians 4, the first ministry Christ gave to the Church was that of the apostle. Literally, an apostle is one who is sent with a specific message to deliver or mission to complete. There are actually two senses in which the ministry of an apostle can and should be considered. First, the term *apostle* was used in a specialized sense in the New Testament. In Acts 1:21,22, the qualifications for apostles were given: (1) They must have been with Jesus from the beginning of His ministry, and (2) they must have been witnesses to the Resurrection. In Ephesians 2:20, apostles are included as part of the foundation upon which the Church is to be built.

Obviously, no one today can meet the qualifications of Acts 1. Similarly, the reference in Ephesians most certainly refers to the original 12 apostles, not to a continual succession of individuals throughout the Church Age. In this specialized sense, there are no apostles today. Yet, in a broader sense, there are!

The Bible describes other individuals as apostles in the church. Even though Paul was not one of the original 12, the New Testament gives ample evidence of his apostleship (Romans 1:1 and 1 Corinthians 9:2, for example). Likewise, Barnabas is referred to as an apostle in Acts 14:4,14. Then, by linking 1 Thessalonians 1:1 with 2:7, it becomes apparent that Paul considered Silas (Silvanus) and Timothy to be apostles.

Returning to the literal meaning of apostle, "one who is sent," Paul, Barnabas, Silas, and Timothy all had one thing in common: They were all missionaries sent by God to another country and culture to proclaim Christ and raise up churches. They did this faithfully. In this broader sense, the ministry of the apostle is seen today in the missionary ranks around the world.

Our own Assemblies of God missionaries have been sent by God to foreign countries to proclaim Jesus Christ and raise up indigenous churches. They are certainly apostles in this broader sense. The vast majority of 20th-century apostles are professional clergy; however, more laypersons are joining the missionary forces around the world each day. We are seeing an increase in the number of "tentmaking" missionaries called by God to spread the gospel. "Tentmakers" are people who go overseas and work at a secular job to support themselves while they do missionary work. Most of these tentmakers are laymen, not credentialed ministers.

2. *Prophet.* The second ministry Paul lists in Ephesians 4:11 is the prophet (see also 1 Corinthians 12:28). The prophet proclaims a divine message, speaking openly to men on behalf of God. In the New Testament churches, prophets formed the foundation for the Church along with the apostles (Ephesians 2:20).

God also has prophets ministering to churches today. He calls men and women and entrusts them with a message to be proclaimed openly, regardless of the consequences. Along with apostles, Christ has placed prophets in the Church to equip or perfect the saints for works of ministry.

The specific role of the prophet today is to warn, awaken, and stir up the Christian community. In doing this, he is not primarily a foreteller or predicter; rather, he is a "forth-teller" of God's Word. He is part of the leadership team Christ has given to His church.

3. *Evangelist.* Paul lists evangelists as the third ministry given by Christ to His church. The evangelist is the messenger of the good news, the gospel. The ministry of the evangelist is to share the gospel with unbelievers in such a way that they become followers of the Lord Jesus Christ.

Philip is the only person specifically called an evangelist in the New Testament (Acts 21:8). His ministry included both preaching and personal witnessing. He preached evangelistically to the people in Samaria (Acts 8:5). They believed and were converted and baptized. As a result, great joy came to Samaria. Shortly after that, God led him to a single Ethiopian traveling in the desert. Philip was just as faithful in proclaiming the gospel to this individual as he had been to the crowds in Samaria. Consequently, the Ethiopian was converted and baptized (Acts 8:37,38).

A study of Christian history reveals many great evangelists throughout the centuries. These were men and women God raised up to proclaim the simple gospel. As a result of their faithfulness, hundreds, thousands, and now millions have been saved. However, this ministry does not end with famous preachers. Paul instructed Timothy, his spiritual son, to "do the work of an evangelist" (2 Timothy 4:5). While Timothy is never specifically called an evangelist, Paul encouraged him to stir up this ministry gift and proclaim the good news.

The evangelist is absolutely necessary in the Church today. The first step in preparing a person to minister for the Lord is to lead him to a personal relationship with Christ. While all Christians are to be witnesses, some are especially enabled by Christ to share the gospel so convincingly that people become followers of Jesus Christ. These men and women are truly evangelists.

God has placed evangelists in every church. They may have neither pulpit nor ministerial credentials, and earn no money from preaching, yet they have a burning desire to share Christ with others, using their God-given ability to share Him effectively.

4. *Pastor-Teacher.* The final ministry Paul mentions in Ephesians 4:11 is the pastor-teacher. Often this ministry is divided into two separate ones, the pastor and the teacher. However, New Testament pastors were to be teachers also.

God has called individuals specifically to pastor a segment of His global church. As pastors, they are expected to care for their congregations in several ways. They are to provide sound Biblical teaching and preaching so the believers will mature in their faith. They are also to minister to the emotional needs of the congregation during times of severe stress or sorrow, bringing the comfort only God can provide.

In looking at the overall ministry of the pastor-teacher, it is not surprising that in the New Testament the words *pastor* and *shepherd* are translations of the same Greek word. Just as the shepherd leads and protects his flock, so the pastor must lead and protect the group of believers entrusted to him by God.

Sometimes a pastor is blessed with one or more individuals in the church who also feel the pastoral call, or burden. These people may never formally become ministers, but they fulfill a vital ministry in the body of Christ as Sunday school teachers, Royal Rangers leaders, youth sponsors, altar workers, and the like. They carry out the "pastoral" ministry God has given them whenever an opportunity arises. When truly led by God, these individuals are never in competition with the staff pastor. Instead, they work in harmony with him, never trying to usurp the authority God and the church have placed in the pastor's hands.

Other Ministry Gifts in the Church

In addition to these four ministries given by Christ to the Church, Paul also refers to other specific ministry gifts. These include helps and service, administrative leadership, giving, and showing mercy.

1. *Helps/Service.* This gift is mentioned in Romans 12:7 and 1 Corinthians 12:28. Generally speaking, it refers to the God-given burden and ability to meet a specific need in the church's mission or operation. Whether this need appears to be critical or trivial, the person having this ministry gift will dedicate himself to see that the need is met. Biblical examples of this gift may be seen in the lives of Onesiphorus (2 Timothy 1:16-18), Epaphroditus (Philippians 2:25,26), Tychicus, and Onesimus (Colossians 4:7,9).

2. *Administrative Leadership.* This ministry gift is mentioned in both Romans 12:8 and 1 Corinthians 12:28. Individ-

uals having this ministry faithfully work to see that the church operates properly. Many times this gift is seen in the pastor's life. If this is not the case, a layman can assist the pastor in this area. This ministry gift was seen in the lives of both Peter and Paul. Paul also implied that it was seen in the leaders of the Ephesian church (Acts 20:28). In the church today, this ministry is essential for proper planning and goal setting. Central to the fulfillment of this ministry is the clear communication of goals and plans to the entire congregation.

3. *Giving.* Every Christian should want to give of his resources to the church. At the same time, God has placed a special burden on the hearts of some people to give continually, generously, even sacrificially, of their resources toward the various ministries of the church. God has called these individuals to the ministry of giving (Romans 12:8). One of the clearest New Testament examples of this ministry gift is seen in the life of Barnabas (Acts 4:36,37). He gave cheerfully of his resources, without being coerced into doing so.

4. *Showing Mercy.* Literally, mercy is the outward manifestation of compassion. While Paul refers to this ministry gift in Romans 12:8, the most apparent New Testament example is in the life of Jesus Christ. Repeatedly, the Gospels state that Jesus had compassion on the people around Him. As a result, He reached out to them and satisfied their needs (e.g., Mark 6:34). Many times the ministry of showing mercy is the least visible one in the church. Genuine mercy is shown in great humility.

Encouraging the Operation of the Gifts

Just as in the case of the gifts of the Spirit, most (if not all) of these ministries can and should be operating in the lives of the members sitting in the pews. Tragically, this is often not the case. Again, the main reasons for this are Satan's opposition to the Church and the general lack of teaching on the subject. The same solutions given in the previous chapter also apply here.

We must realize we are in spiritual warfare against Satan and his kingdom. In recognizing this, the Christian should lean on the Lord and desire to be used by God. This sensitivity will, in turn, lead to a greater desire for teaching and involvement in the ministries of the church. The church must be prepared to provide this teaching.

This program of teaching can be from the pulpit or in the Sunday school classroom. It should include topics such as (1) the believer's responsibility to the church, (2) available opportunities for ministries in the church, and (3) specific guidance in the Christian's involvement in these ministries.

The first two topics are fairly clear. The third one should include special qualifications needed for the various ministry opportunities. It should also include an explanation of how a believer can determine which area of ministry is best for him. This process of determination begins with a critical self-evaluation. The individual should review the talents and special abilities God has given him. He should also consider which areas of church service interest him most. While this is not an infallible indicator, it can show the beginnings of a God-given burden for a particular area of ministry in the church.

In many ways, the pastor is the key to the involvement of the laity in the ministries of the local church. When the pastor supports and encourages the church members to become involved, they usually will do so. On the other hand, if the members receive neither teaching nor encouragement, they will never become fully involved, and the church will not grow as it should.

The importance of this teaching and the role of the pastor will be discussed in greater detail in the remaining chapters.

7

The Energy Crisis

Having laid a Biblical basis for training lay ministers, we will now address some practical concerns. We will answer questions like, How do we equip the saints for ministry? How do people discover their spiritual gifts? How can we help new Christians achieve maturity? Do problems develop when much emphasis is placed on the personal ministry of each believer? How are churches implementing lay ministry training programs now?

In this chapter we want to address a critical concern many Christian leaders face: an energy crisis. It is far more critical than oil or gas shortages that many nations are facing. This is a matter of eternity. Jesus described this shortage when He said, "The harvest truly is plenteous, but the laborers are few" (Matthew 9:37).

The same seems to be still true. Our world is wide open to receive the gospel. People everywhere are trying everything they can think of to find peace, joy, hope, and fulfillment in life. In the United States we have liberty to take the gospel to every person through means unavailable and unknown to past generations. The Holy Spirit is moving in unprecedented ways. Local churches are larger now than at any time in our history. Our churches are sitting in the middle of a ripened harvest field. But where are the workers?

Most churches have many more adults uninvolved in ministry than actively involved. It would be easy to point an accusing finger in several directions. We could blame the church member in the pew. We could blame the pastor and other leaders. We could blame the fast pace of our society, saying, "People are just too busy to become involved in the Lord's work." But let's not blame anyone. Let's look at some solutions. Let's consider some possibilities.

Most of our churches fall into one of the three categories described in the following quotations:

1. "Many are being saved and are attending our church. In fact, there are so many that we don't know what to do."
2. "Many are coming to us from other churches, often hungry for the infilling of the Holy Spirit. They enjoy our worship services, but it is hard to get them and others involved."
3. "Very little to nothing is happening. Few, if any, are being saved from year to year. We seem to lose what few we do get. Many of us are discouraged. It seems like just a few of us really care; just a few are doing anything. We are getting tired."

It doesn't matter whether your church is a home missions church or a well-established church, these situations may exist. How do we help new converts become mature and encourage them to grow into the image of Christ? (Romans 8:29).

Let's consider some stages in the development of a Christian's life. When a person receives Jesus Christ as his Saviour and Lord, he becomes a son of God, a *convert*. Then the believer becomes a *disciple*, a learner or convinced adherent of Christ. As his relationship with God grows, he becomes a *minister* of Christ for "the perfecting of saints, for the work of the ministry, for the edifying of the body of Christ" (Ephesians 4:12). The believer eventually becomes a *trainer* of others for service to Christ. "The things that thou hast heard . . . commit thou to faithful men, who shall be able to teach others also (2 Timothy 2:2).

Christian Development

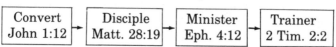

Discipling

Once people are saved, the church has a continuing responsibility to them. It is our task to disciple them. Jesus commanded, "Go therefore and make disciples of all the nations" (Matthew 28:19, NKJV). A disciple is a convinced adherent. At least three ingredients are necessary in order to make a disciple: Biblical teaching, Christian models, and fellowship with the Body.

New Christians must have sound Biblical teaching, beginning at the time of conversion. They need to know the plan of salvation: Christ died for their sins; their sins are covered through the blood sacrifice of the Lord; they have received Christ by faith, not by feeling.

At New Life Assembly in Athens, this teaching was continued in two ways. First, we enrolled them in our ongoing new Christians class, The Discovery of a Lifetime. They received at least three invitations and encouragements to be part of that class the next Sunday after their conversion. In the class they were taught basic Biblical truths. We used several resources, primarily *First Things First*, edited by Keith H. Parks (Lay Leadership Institute, Inc. ©1981, 1267 Hicks Blvd., Fairfield, OH 45014). This fine study booklet is written specifically for the new convert. A number of other resources are also available.

Second, we assigned a discipler to each new Christian. The discipler kept in personal contact with the convert to help answer questions and ground him in scriptural growth. Since man does not live by "bread alone, but by every Word that proceedeth out of the mouth of God" (Matthew 4:4), each new Christian needs to be taught the Scriptures immediately.

Some may say, "We don't have a new Christians class because we don't have enough new Christians." All you need is one new convert to start a class. "But we don't have *any* new Christians!" Very likely you will not have any until you are ready for them. Most married couples I know prepare the nursery in their home before the child is delivered. They make ready the crib and changing table. When the child is born the proud parents take the baby to the beautifully prepared nursery. That is exactly what we need to do in the church: Get the spiritual nursery ready; prepare for the new Christians. Then we are ready for God to save souls and entrust them to us.

New Christians, in order to be disciples, must have a model. This model should be a Christian who is stable, consistent, and has good spiritual habits. He will model how to overcome temptation, how to pray, how to read the Word, how to witness, how to handle job and family pressures. In reality the new Christian will follow that model as the model follows Christ.

New Christians also need fellowship with the body of Christ in order to become disciples. Of course, fellowship occurs in many ways. Having an older Christian as a discipler/model will provide fellowship. Attending the church services and activities of the local church will provide some fellowship. However, the best fellowship I know of is being a part of a small home group.

My wife, Debbie, and I were part of a small home fellowship with several people in our church. We ate together, studied together, sang Christmas carols together, laughed together, and cried together. That is fellowship. All Christians need such a place with freedom to ask questions, request prayer, express fears, shed tears, receive encouragement, and give and receive love. That is hard to do with a group of more than 12 to 15 people. The Early Church met in homes as well as in large group settings. We need to rediscover the joy and blessing of this practice.

Ministering

As this process of discipleship continues, we then begin to move toward the third step: ministry. Discipleship and ministry go hand in hand. Part of the discipling process is learning how to minister. Saints cannot be equipped through truth alone. They are not equipped until they serve. *Equipped saints are serving saints.*

It is at this point that each pastor and local church must develop a plan to involve each person, new Christian or otherwise, in ministry within the church. In the next chapter we will consider some possible models for equipping the saints to minister.

Training

Finally, the process of development continues as each Christian moves from serving as a minister to serving as a trainer. Paul told Timothy, "The things you have heard me say in the presence of many witnesses entrust to reliable men who will also be qualified to teach others" (2 Timothy 2:2, NIV). As these new Christians grow into spiritual maturity and Christ-likeness through ministering, they will become ready to train others. They have been discipled and taught, and now they begin the process with someone else. Hence the cycle is complete and begins all over again.

A mature church will have many trainers. This continued process gives purpose and meaning to many saints who have been attending church for a long time. They may feel that their lives and experiences are no longer needed in the church. Yet they are a ready-made reservoir of trainers to instruct new Christians in general spiritual growth and/or provide specific training for specific ministries.

Finishing the Master's Work

Regardless of your church's position in its growth and development, you can begin to meet the needs of this energy crisis. Involve as many people as possible in one of these four ongoing stages of Christian development. You will always have converts, disciples, ministers, and trainers. The process goes on and on.

The story is told of a great composer, Giacomo Puccini, whose operas number among the world's favorites—*Tosca, La Boheme, Madame Butterfly*. Even after he was stricken with cancer in 1922, Puccini was determined to write a final opera,

Turandot, which some consider his best. Fighting the awful cancer, Puccini was implored by his students to rest, to save his strength. But he persisted, remarking at one point, "If I do not finish my music, my students will finish it."

In 1924 Puccini was taken to Brussels for an operation. He died there 2 days after his surgery. His students did finish *Turandot* and in 1926 the gala premiere was held in the magnificent La Scala Opera House in Milan, Italy, under the baton of Puccini's favorite student, Arturo Toscanini.

All went brilliantly that evening until they came to the point in the score where the teacher had been obliged to put down his pen. Toscanini, his face wet with tears, stopped the production, put down his baton, turned to the audience, and cried out, "Thus far the master wrote, but he died." After a few minutes, his face now wreathed in smiles, Toscanini picked up his baton and cried out to the audience, "But his disciples finished his work."

That's an inspiring story. Unfortunately, at the point of inspiration, it's not true. Yes, *Turandot* was finished by another composer, Franco Alfano. Yes, its premiere was at La Scala, Milan. And, yes, Arturo Toscanini, a student of Puccini, did conduct. However, according to *Music Since 1900* by Nicolas Slonimsky, Toscanini conducted *Turandot* "up to the last measure written by Puccini himself, omitting Alfano's ending."

The disciples of Christ must not omit the ending intended by the Master. When Christ returned to the Father, He left a mission for us to bring to completion. We are to finish His work of converting, discipling, ministering, and training others to do so, "until He comes."

The laborers are few. But by following what we have shared in this chapter, and by putting into action an "equipping plan," such as we shall discuss in the next chapter, we can begin to solve this energy crisis.

8

Models for Equipping for Ministry

"God intends each believer to be an agent of God's Kingdom in the ordinariness of his life." This statement by Jack Hayford, one of America's leading pastors, should challenge pastors and other Christian leaders to take seriously their responsibility to equip the saints to do the work of the ministry. All of us who are in full-time Christian service must recognize that if our people, the people of God, are going to accept their responsibility to minister, then the clergy must become enablers, equipping them for ministry.

What does it mean to "equip the saints"? As stated earlier, it means "to perfect" them, "to fit or prepare fully." Availability does not equal capability. While God certainly wants us to be available, He also wants us to be equipped. James Garlow, in his classic book *Partners in Ministry*, comments,

> Over the past few years I have observed numerous churches and their training programs. I am convinced that in many local churches, training laypersons for their ministry is an extremely low priority. . . . Lay training must be intentional. Much of what has been labeled lay training has been done by default rather than by design. Lay ministry needs to happen "on purpose." It must be designed with clear objectives, goals, and methods.[1]

There is an ever-growing number of pastors and churches who are keenly aware that lay training must be intentional. They have designed equipping and training programs to assist their people in finding their own place in the ministry of the church. In this way they can further affect their world. Our hope is that, as you read the following synopses of other churches' programs, the Holy Spirit will begin to show you how your church can carry on an aggressive and purposeful equipping and training ministry.

Ravenna, Ohio

While Rev. Bruno Glodkowski pastored Ravenna Assembly of God, he saw the need to prepare the saints for ministry. He carried on his program for nearly 2 years before resigning to become the Ohio district's director of Christian education. The name of the Ravenna program was Equipping the Church (ETC). The stated goal was "To take new believers and incorporate them into the local church."

This particular ministry started rather simply and evolved into a more comprehensive program as the pastoral staff, headed by Pastor Glodkowski, saw the needs. It began with a newcomers Sunday school class taught by the pastor. The class lasted 9 months. The pastor taught basic Biblical truths, such as salvation, the baptism in the Holy Spirit, and the personal ministry of each believer. Although this class was very helpful, more instruction was needed.

They then started the second stage, a leadership class taught by one of the associate pastors. Those whom Pastor Glodkowski saw had leadership potential, from his observations during the first 9 months, were invited and encouraged to enroll in the leadership class. This class, which also met during the Sunday school hour, lasted 6 months. The curriculum dealt with the qualities of leadership.

Following this 6 months of training, the students had a further opportunity for another 6 months of Sunday school study on "life-style" evangelism. They felt still more was needed. The Sunday school format continued, and a Wednesday evening training session was added. A 6- to 10-week program of electives on Wednesday evening was established. Classes were taught by the pastoral staff and qualified laymen on subjects such as spiritual gifts, music skills, and how to study the Bible.

To reach the entire church body, Pastor Glodkowski preached two Sunday morning sermons each June on the subject of Body ministry. Following the sermon on the second Sunday of this series, each person in attendance received a ministry inventory, entitled "Mobilization for Service." Each individual was asked to sign up to be involved in a ministry through the local church. For Ravenna Assembly of God, ETC was an umbrella for their entire lay training ministry. It involved Sunday school, Sunday morning sermons, and Wednesday evenings.

According to Brother Glodkowski, the results were rewarding. He noted that a large percentage of the people became integrally involved in the church. In fact "approximately 70-75 percent of those who went through both the Newcomers Class and the Leadership Class became and remained active in the church."

Even though Pastor Glodkowski is no longer at Ravenna, the concept of ETC remains uppermost in the mind of his successor. To strengthen the leadership, an intensive weekend training program now occurs each quarter. In addition, five Sunday school classes are being offered to disciple and equip the saints for ministry.

Springfield, Missouri

At Evangel Temple in Springfield, Missouri, an exciting equipping program has been started and continues to develop. In September 1982, Pastor Cal LeMon began Springfield Salt and Light Company. This training program has two primary objectives: First, "to train people to serve as lay pastors." These lay pastors have the responsibility for a "people parish," which consists of six family units or less. These "parishes" meet at least once a month for prayer, fellowship, and support. The second objective of their program is "to train people for leadership responsibilities in the church," such as those of an elder or Sunday school teacher.

The program is primarily centered around a Wednesday evening training session. For 9 months, Pastor LeMon teaches on a number of subjects, including how to lead someone to Christ, how to counsel (grief, marriage, personal, etc.), discovering spiritual gifts, public speaking, time management, and leadership. They strongly encourage the participants not to miss more than five times in the 9-month period.

Pastor LeMon says the results are evident. The people are more spiritually mature, and many have taken on responsibilities for ministry. As they review this ministry, the leadership is contemplating making the training a 4-month program, rather than continuing the current 9-month format.

Bell Gardens, California

The Full Gospel Assembly of God, under Colman McDuff's pastoral leadership, is experiencing "Pentecostal revival" which he attributes directly to their lay training concept, called Full Gospel School of Ministry.

The emphasis of their training is character training: "having an in-depth encounter with the character of Jesus transfused into the hearts of the people, which in turn results in discovering their ministry and where they function best in the body of Christ." Pastor McDuff comments, "When one is reflecting the inner character of Christ, you feel safe in releasing him for ministry."

Their method is a cell approach called Discipleship Through Relationships. Using material and other helps prepared by Lay Leadership International, their in-house training cells meet on Monday evenings in various parts of the church building. From 150 to 180 attend each week, meeting in individual cells of 9 to 12 people, each with a trained leader. They began this concept in March 1980, and it continues for 30 weeks out of the year. Six levels of training are offered, each level lasting 10 weeks. Over a 2-year period all six levels may be gone through.

Pastor McDuff shared that "discovering Kingdom character (the Beatitudes) in a Kingdom setting (discipleship through relationships) brings on a Kingdom explosion (Pentecost)." That is exactly what is happening there. Leadership is being developed to the degree that 98 percent of the leadership for all areas in the church now come through their School of Ministry.

The pastor is very much involved. He has personally trained most of the leaders and continues to train new leaders. He noted that a ministry like this "*must* grow out of the heart of the pastor. Jesus did not leave the discipling process up to Peter, James, and John. He did it *himself.* The pastor *must* get involved; he is the *key!*"

Adrian, Michigan

In Adrian, Michigan, Bethany Assembly of God is thriving. Pastored by William F. Leach, this church sets the pace for many other churches in Michigan, especially with regard to their Sunday school, Royal Rangers, and Missionettes ministries. At the helm of those ministries, giving direction and encouragement, is Robert Burkhart, the associate pastor responsible for the Christian education programs. A number of years ago Pastor Burkhart recognized that if the church was going to adequately staff its various programs as they grew, a recruiting and training strategy had to be developed. What follows was developed by Pastor Burkhart for Bethany Assembly of God.

They title their ongoing program "Pre-Ministry Training." This equipping program, which has continued every quarter since September 1981, has three goals:
1. To provide a sufficient, well-equipped staff for all the Christian education ministries of the church.
2. To provide believers who are not in ministry with an opportunity to discover, develop, and use their spiritual gifts.
3. To provide a growing staff at predictable rates and intervals in order to replace staff losses and to allow for the creation of new units.

Bethany's Pre-Ministry Training takes place during the Sunday school hour and has three phases.

In phase 1, which lasts 9 weeks, different subjects are taught, such as every member ministry, spiritual gifts, the role of the church in your ministry, outreach, qualification and role, and organization and structure. The last week of this phase is Commitment Week.

Phase 2 is 4 weeks in length and is designed for those who are going into any teaching ministry of the church. In this period the students are taught principles of teaching. Those who are going into Sunday school, Royal Rangers, Missionettes, or any other teaching ministry will participate in this phase. Those who are not going into a teaching ministry may move directly into phase 3.

Phase 3 is an 8-week internship program. Regardless of the ministry to which the persons are committing themselves, they must be involved in this phase. The first 2 weeks are spent in observation. In the next 4 weeks, members are given partial responsibility. In the last 2 weeks the new recruit has the full responsibility for that ministry, under the watchful eye of a mentor.

Pastor Burkhart stated during a recent interview that their Pre-Ministry Training has been effective. Not only have they met their stated goals, but the people have been challenged spiritually to examine their relationship to God and the calling of God on their lives. Further, the 225 who have completed this training have a greater appreciation for their local church.

The materials for the program used at Bethany have been published and may be obtained from Gospel Light Publications, Ventura, California. The *Teacher Training Manual* contains everything needed to implement this ministry in your church. Specific questions may be addressed to Pastor Rob Burkhart in Adrian, Michigan.

Athens, Ohio

A description of the Equipping for Ministry training program used in Athens, Ohio, was given in the first chapter of this book. Some additional details are included here to provide a capsule view of this program.

Our stated goal was simply to "mobilize every adult and teenager in our church into at least one active ministry." Naturally, that has been refined and developed since, but that was our initial thrust. We use a 13-week format during the Sunday school hour. We have both specific recruiting and open enrollment for the class. I personally contact people I know are saved and reasonably well-grounded in their Christian faith, encouraging them to sign up for the class.

Another source of member enrollment is the new converts class of the church. After an individual completes 3 or 6 months in the new converts class, we encourage him to become involved in the Equipping for Ministry Class. The class size varies from quarter to quarter, ranging from 10 to about 25 in each cycle.

The course is divided into three sections. Section 1 contains four lessons, "Every Person a Minister," "The Church," "A Biblical Study on Spiritual Gifts," and "The Parable of the Talents." Those lessons cover 6 weeks.

In section 2 the various spiritual gifts are defined and explained in great detail. Included in this section also is the use of a "Spiritual Gifts Inventory," which each student completes at home. This takes place about the 10th week. The "Spiritual Gifts Inventory" worksheet was developed specifically for our class and includes features from several of the inventories available from other sources. Two weeks later, the students are given a "Commitment to Ministry" form that covers all the possible ministries available in the church.

Section 3 is the practical application. This consists of a personal interview with the teacher. During this interview the student shares what the class has meant to him or her. Then the teacher looks at the "Spiritual Gifts Inventory" results and discusses them with the student. The teacher stresses that the inventory is simply a tool to help a person begin discovering his gifts and strengths. At that point, the student makes a commitment to become involved in a specific area of ministry. The "Commitment to Ministry" form is then completed and signed. The interview concludes with prayer, asking the Lord to grant the student success in the ministry in which he or she will become involved.

With the commitment in hand, the teacher makes contact with the leader of the ministry to which that person has just committed himself. The leader of that ministry then makes contact with the new recruit and the second stage begins. This person is then given specialized training for that specific ministry by the leader of that ministry. This stage is very important. Enthusiasm will quickly wane if the person is left to discover for himself how to fulfill his ministry.

This equipping ministry is still in its developmental stages. Revisions are always being made. Recently a student manual was printed and bound, a copy of which is given to each student on the first day of class. This workbook gives the general outline for the class and allows the student to take notes each week, enhancing the learning process.

The results of this young program have been encouraging. A full 75 percent of those who have completed this 13-week class through 1984 were involved in a ministry through the church at that time. The church hopes to eventually have every adult in the church take the Equipping for Ministry Class and maintain a 75-percent involvement rate in lay ministry. Materials for the course "Equipping for Ministry" are available from New Life Assembly, Athens, Ohio.

Equipping Programs Similarities

Although each of these five equipping programs is different, reflecting the needs of each church and the philosophy of its pastor, several commonalities should be noted:

1. The pastor was the key to the birth of the program in each case. In four of the five instances, the pastor teaches a major segment, if not all of the program. The pastor also complements this ministry by regularly emphasizing the value and importance of lay ministry through his sermons.

2. In each case, some time was given to the study of spiritual gifts. Only by understanding the purpose of spiritual gifts will the church member begin to see his place in the work of the Lord.
3. In each case, commitments were asked for and received. Opportunity must be given for the individuals to commit themselves to a specific ministry.
4. Specific training is available, and often required, once a commitment has been made to a particular ministry.
5. In three of the five instances, the Sunday school hour was used as either the exclusive or the primary time for teaching.

It is not too late to start. Begin now to seek the Lord, asking Him to give you a specific plan for your church. "Start where you are; use what you have; do what you can." Begin and let it grow.

------

[1]James Garlow, *Partners in Ministry* (Kansas City, MO: Beacon Hill, 1981), p. 104.

9

The Equipping Process

Equipping the saints for ministry is really not a difficult process, but neither are there any shortcuts. Equipping is more than a few Bible lessons, a spiritual gifts inventory, and some training. Paul underscores this in Ephesians 4:1-16. He offers eight truths vital to understanding the equipping process.

The Christian's Calling

Equipping begins with our calling. In writing to the Ephesians, Paul urges them to "live a life worthy of the calling you have received" (4:1, NIV). Every Christian has a calling. It is a high and holy calling, and we are to live a life that is worthy of that kind of calling.

We say, "Praise the Lord, tonight John was called into the ministry!" What we probably mean is that tonight the Lord called John to become a pastor or a missionary, and John will probably go to Bible college to prepare for this ministry. We must remind ourselves that every Christian has been called. Responding to God's particular call in our lives will lead us in different directions; nevertheless, we are all called.

The Christian's Character

Second, that calling for all of us is to a life of character. Paul says, "Be completely humble and gentle; be patient, bearing with one another in love" (4:2, NIV). No amount of training and motivation will be sufficient if a person's life is without character. One of the important tasks of the local church leaders is to help the people in the congregation develop a life consistent with the character of Jesus and His kingdom.

After Christ called His disciples, He began to teach them the nature of the Kingdom. Through this they began to encounter the character of Christ. It's outlined for us in the Beatitudes (Matthew 5:3-12). The character of Christ is one of humility, a broken heart, a thirst for righteousness, an attitude of mercy, a pure heart, a desire to make peace, and a willingness to suffer wrong for His sake.

Any equipping process that leaves out character is short-cutting the Biblical process. Part of the goal of equipping the saints is making disciples. Disciples are those who reflect the inner character of Jesus Christ.

The Christian's Unity

The third step in the equipping process mentioned by Paul is unity. Christians who have the character of Christ, the fruit of the Spirit, forming in their lives will undoubtedly live in peace and unity with each other.

Carnality breeds disunity. Paul wrote to the Corinthians, "For ye are yet carnal: for whereas there is among you envying, and strife and divisions, are ye not carnal, and walk as men?" (1 Corinthians 3:3). On the other hand, those who have the character traits of Christ will be in unity. There is "one Lord, one faith, one baptism, one God and Father of all" (Ephesians 4:5,6). Just as there is unity in the Godhead, there should be unity in His church.

The Christian's Gift

The fourth step in the equipping process is recognizing and understanding the gifts God has given to His church. Though there is one Lord, one faith, one Baptism, one God and Father, there are many gifts (see Ephesians 4:5-7). When Christ ascended, He gave gifts to the Church so we could continue His work on earth. No one is excluded.

Peter says it: "Each one has received a gift" (1 Peter 4:10,

NKJV). Each child of God will be used by the Lord in at least one spiritual gift. Each of God's children is gifted. Only a few, comparatively speaking, will have the "equipment" gifts of apostle, prophet, evangelist, and pastor-teacher. Far more, in fact the overwhelming majority, will have one or more of the "service" gifts. Of course, any yielded, Spirit-filled believer can be an instrument through whom the Holy Spirit will show himself through one of the nine "manifestation" gifts.

Paul noted that Christ ascended "in order to fill the whole universe" (Ephesians 4:10, NIV). He fills the universe with His Spirit, to be sure. That is why He could say, "Where two or three are gathered together in my name there am I in the midst of them" (Matthew 18:20). But the Lutherans have a thought worth considering (more properly in another context, it is true): the universality of Christ's body.[1] Although we believers, the body of Christ, do not fill the universe, we should be salt and light wherever we are. We become effective in that way by understanding our calling, possessing the character of Christ, living in unity, and ministering with the gifts we have been entrusted with.

The Christian's Ministry

The fifth step in the equipping process is understanding that the gifts of the Spirit are given for ministry, for service to others. The gift is not an end in itself, only a means to an end. The end is ministry, touching people for the Lord. Frankly, the world does not care which gifts we have, or what we call them, or how we categorize them. Hurting people want to know: "Does she care? Will he help? Can she help? Are they too busy for me? Do they have the compassion and love of Jesus?"

Peter, in his message to Cornelius' household and friends, touched on this, "how God anointed Jesus of Nazareth with the Holy Ghost and with power: who went about doing good, and healing all that were oppressed of the devil; for God was with him" (Acts 10:38). The proof of the power of the Holy Spirit in Jesus' life was not a piece of paper listing all the gifts He had.

Rather, it was that He ministered with the anointing of the Spirit of the Lord. He healed, He taught, He delivered, He befriended, He cared. God gave the four "equipment" gifts of apostle, prophet, evangelist, and pastor-teacher for one purpose—to prepare God's people to minister.

The Christian's Edification

The sixth step in the equipping process is edification (Ephesians 4:12). As the perfected saints minister, the church is edified, or built up. Many of us want to be edified, but this does not come immediately. It follows when Christians understand their calling, possess the character of Christ, live in unity, understand their gifts, and minister to one another in those gifts. Then the church cannot help but be edified. However, edification is not the final goal.

The Christian's Maturity

The seventh step in the equipping process is maturity. The church must not only be edified, but mature as well, attaining "the whole measure of the fullness of Christ" (4:13, NIV). This maturity is evidenced by stability, doctrinal soundness, and Christlikeness. How Christ must yearn for maturity in His church, maturity that will keep us from dividing over petty issues—or even over major ones.

The Christian's Growth

The final stage in the equipping process is growth (4:16, NIV). God never intended that His church become edified and mature, and then sit back, rest, and wait for His return. The Great Commission is still in force: "Go and make disciples of all nations" (Matthew 28:19, NIV).

We all want growth. Every layman, every pastor, every evangelist wants to see it. But why aren't some of our churches growing? Some pastors say, "We're growing spiritually but not numerically." The Scriptures indicate that the outgrowth of a spiritually growing (maturing) body is numerical growth. The body, according to Ephesians 4:16, grows as a result of the equipping process.

What happens when a church begins to live by Ephesians 4:1-16, putting this eight-step equipping process into practice? It begins to grow. And it will make an impact on its world. People will be saved, filled with the Holy Spirit, and become like Jesus Christ. Church members and leaders will be too busy to feud over the color of the carpet or the maintenance of the new van. Instead, they will find people they never knew were there, people who are hungry for real Christianity.

There are no shortcuts to this equipping process. Don't try to do it all tomorrow. Rather, let the Holy Spirit make these truths real to you. Consider the needs of your church in prayer, and ask God for specific direction. Take some of these models and pray about them. Allow the creative Holy Spirit to give you a plan that is just right for your church.

---

[1]Charles Hodge, *A Commentary on the Epistle to the Ephesians* (Grand Rapids: Baker Book House, 1980), p. 222.

10

Obstacles and Rewards

Recently, I heard a sermon by a friend, Pastor Dave Gable, who grew up under my father's ministry in Pennsylvania. In this message he gave some helpful teaching about gifts from the Old Testament story of David and Goliath. He also shared some principles for finding and using your spiritual gifts.

Start With the Holy Spirit

Jesse's son David was first aware of his ministry when Samuel anointed him with oil (a symbol of the Holy Spirit). He was still a shepherd and an unlikely candidate for king. Neither his family nor Samuel suspected that David was God's choice for king of Israel. "The Lord seeth not as man seeth; for man looketh on the outward appearance, but the Lord looketh on the heart" (1 Samuel 16:7). We, too, must start with the Holy Spirit. We dare not start with books, inventories, classes, or seminars. We must begin with prayer, allowing the Holy Spirit to anoint us for the work He is calling us to do, even if that work is unknown to us at the time.

Sometimes we want to know what our gift is before we do anything for the Lord. This can put us under bondage. Often, as we do the things God puts in front of us to do, our gifts will be discovered. David went to visit his brothers, who had gone with Saul to battle. There he found Goliath defying God's armies. And all the men of Israel fled. No one confronted Goliath (1 Samuel 17). But David saw something—he saw a man speaking against God. Fresh from the anointing, David felt a stirring within him. He said, "I've got to do something." David began to be aware of a potential gift.

You will never know what your gift is if you don't try. Whether it's fixing a leak, building a house, cutting down a tree, sharing Christ, or running the sound system at church, it is a great feeling to know God will use you to minister to the Body.

Move Ahead by Trial and Error

Would David find Saul's armor to his delight or to his disappointment? It's good to expose ourselves to different kinds of Christian ministry. In this way we gain a deeper appreciation for others. David went to Saul and offered his services to kill Goliath. David tried on Saul's armor to see if it would fit, but it didn't. Dave Gable said, "I like David's willingness to try the armor. And I like David's wisdom to know it didn't fit." I often told individuals who had completed the Equipping for Ministry course at New Life, "Go ahead and try it if you'd like. If it doesn't work out, let's pray and try something else."

God spoke to Moses, and asked, "What is that in your hand?" (Exodus 4:2, NIV). God used Moses' rod for many miracles. He used a little boy's lunch to feed a multitude. He used plain water in pitchers to meet the need of a host at a wedding and save him from embarrassment. God used the sling in David's hand. David had used that sling on many previous occasions, but now it was God's instrument. God would love to use for His glory some of the natural skills you've developed over the years.

Keep Your Focus on God

After David laid down Saul's armor and picked up his sling, he spoke to Saul, "The *Lord* that delivered me out of the paw of the lion, and out of the paw of the bear, he will deliver me out of the hand of this Philistine" (1 Samuel 17:37, italics mine). David made no mention of the sling, although it was in his hand. His hope was in God. Then, when he faced Goliath in the field, he shouted triumphantly, "Thou comest to me with a sword, and with a spear, and with a shield: but I come to thee in the name of the *Lord* of hosts, the *God* of the armies of Israel, whom thou hast defied" (17:45, italics mine). Though he had gifts, he focused on the strength and deliverance of God. What a lesson!

So often we focus on our strengths or weaknesses. We swell with pride as we think of how good our gift is, or we shrink with disappointment and embarrassment as we comtemplate our insufficiencies. Frankly, our weaknesses and insufficiencies are not very important, and neither are our strengths. What is important on the battlefield of life is this: Are we focusing on God, the gift giver? This doesn't mean that we forget the gift, or that we leave it at home. No, we take all the resources the Lord has given us; then we allow Him to direct their use. Our gifts are servants to the Giver.

David killed Goliath with a sling, but he didn't say, "The sling and stone are all I'll ever need." God used the sling one day and the sword the next. God may want to use you one way today, and another way tomorrow. The day David killed Goliath he was a warrior. Another day he was a leader of men, an administrator, a king. David didn't lock into one thing forever. Neither did he insist that everyone else in Israel should use the sling and stone. God worked a great victory that day because he had a young man in touch with the Holy Spirit, who recognized his gift and moved ahead by trial and error, allowing God to use his natural skill for a supernatural purpose. His eyes were focused on His God, and the enemy was defeated.

Lay Ministry in the Local Church

We face other enemies that need to be defeated, and they are not always outside the camp. Sometimes they are among us. Fears and doubts surface when we begin to talk about releasing saints to minister within the church. Pastors sometimes become very nervous. Laymen can become a bit jittery, too. "Me, what can *I* do? I'm just a layman." There are some obstacles we ought to address and not hide.

Some pastors will feel threatened at the thought of lay ministry, but when the equipping process is patterned after the one built on Ephesians 4:1-16, with unity in the Body, any threat to the pastor is minimized. At the base of the process is Christian character. When members of the church strive for unity, no one will be out to usurp the pastor's authority. Even if someone would try, other members of the church would defend the pastor. Laymen can also help minimize any threat by letting their pastor and other church leaders know that they are dependent on the pastor and his staff for their training.

Some pastors may feel inadequate to provide training in lay ministry. That is certainly understandable. The best thing for the pastor to do is admit his feeling of inadequacy. Any attempt to hide it and plow ahead will result in the lessening of confidence in his leadership among the congregation. Instead, one must admit his need; seek the Lord; call on others; then do his best. Many pastors were not taught how to train others. Many of us know nothing about delegation of authority and job descriptions. We are learning as we go. The best thing for the layman to do is to be patient with the pastor. As the laymen are patient, the pastor will grow more confident and develop skills in this vital area.

Some pastors may feel that lay training is unnecessary. Although very few would say that "equipping the saints to do the work of the ministry" is unscriptural, for some it is very low on their ministerial priority list. Laymen have a difficult task if they are under a pastor who will not become involved with lay ministry training. Pray for him; share your concern with him. Don't start a get-rid-of-the-pastor crusade. Be patient, trusting that the Lord will help him to see the need.

On the other hand, some laymen feel threatened at the thought of lay ministry. Many times the layman's attitude is, "Let the pastor do it! That's what he is paid for!" Some people are frightened at the prospect of ministering. What should the pastor do? Begin with those who are ready, while continuing to work patiently and lovingly with those who feel threatened by it. He should not force them, but lead them. Generally they will follow. If you are a layman who feels threatened at the thought of ministry, admit your fear or other concern. Maybe you feel you have failed in the past and do not want to try again. Share that with your pastor and allow him to help you as you begin. Don't let fear paralyze you and keep you from being all that you can be in the Lord. You are gifted for ministry in God's kingdom. You are needed. Just start slowly.

Some laymen may feel inadequate as lay ministers. This should not be a surprise. After all, most people have had absolutely no training for any Christian work. An inadequate feeling is normal. Don't interpret that feeling as an unwillingness to cooperate or to work for the Lord. Be willing to be led. The Holy Spirit will help.

Layperson, if you are feeling unsure, take heart. Remember, though, that in your weakness God can make you strong. "My grace is sufficient for thee: for my strength is made perfect in weakness" (2 Corinthians 12:9). Do your best and God will surely do the rest.

Some laypersons may feel that training is unnecessary. There probably aren't too many in this category. But when you find one, Pastor, most of the time it is best to let him go ahead and minister without the training. It is hard to fill a need if the person doesn't think he has one. Eventually he may come to an awareness of his need for more training.

Occasionally you will find a person who legitimately needs no training. He really knows how to minister in a particular area. Perhaps he could be used in helping others to learn. If you as a layperson feel that training for you is unnecessary, please—for the sake of the body of Christ—cooperate with the training program. Show the fruit of meekness, and submit to God-ordained leadership.

In addition to those obstacles, be aware of these potential problems:

1. *Rationalization.* "I've got my gift so I don't need to do anything else for the Lord. I'll just do my own thing."

2. *Self-deception.* This is the one who thinks he has a gift, but doesn't.

3. *Guilt.* "I can't seem to discover my gift; there must be something wrong with me." Whatever we do, we can't allow the enemy to heap guilt on a person who is sincerely seeking the Lord's will. The answer: Begin to minister in an area that looks interesting and challenging to you. Sometimes you'll find your gift as a result of your ministering.

4. *Pride.* "My gift is more important than your gift." Remember it is not *your* gift or *my* gift. It is the *Holy Spirit's* gift. Also, don't judge the value of the gift by how much recognition it receives. The noticed gifts are not any more important than those that are less noticed.

5. *Gift projection.* "If I can sing in the choir, then anyone can." This simply is not true. And even if someone else has natural singing talent, it does not automatically follow that God wants him to minister through music. When we project our gift on someone else, we are assuming the *Spirit's* role of leading people. We also place false guilt on that person if he doesn't agree with our assumption.

Now let us turn to the rewards of an equipped church and of its individual members. These rewards of following God's plan and mobilizing His people for ministry far outweigh any problems that may surface.

Rewards of Lay Ministry

Jesus talked about rewards in the Parable of the Talents (Matthew 25:14-30). The judgment is severe for hiding the talent, but the reward is great for using the talents wisely:

1. Christ *commends* us: "Well done, good and faithful servant" (Matthew 25:23).

2. Christ *promotes* us: "Thou hast been faithful over a few things, I will make thee ruler over many things" (Matthew 25:21,23).

3. Christ *invites* us: "Enter thou into the joy of thy Lord" (Matthew 25:21,23).

First, each Christian finds his place in the church. "God set the members every one of them in the body, as it hath pleased him" (1 Corinthians 12:18). It is a great feeling to know where you fit in, and how you best contribute to, the body of Christ. A football player will be very anxious and not nearly as productive if he doesn't know or cannot accept his place on the team. On the field, there is a place for only one quarterback. Several ends and a couple of running backs are vital to the success of the offense. Then there are the "big horses," the offensive linemen, who seldom run with the football. Very few people know their names. But they just push ahead, making room for the players who carry the ball. When a lineman understands his role, how he fits into the overall scheme of things, he will contribute to the team's success and be effective.

At the conclusion of the Sunday school class Equipping for Ministry (to which I referred earlier) I met with each student for a consultation about how he fit into the local church. What a joy it was when a man or woman would say, "You mean I can do that for the Lord!" What a relief and joy to know we fit into the body of Christ, into our local church.

The second reward of discovering, developing, and deploying our spiritual gift is that each member of the church works together more effectively. My hand, eye, ear, and nose are not working competitively, but cooperatively. That makes for a more effective functioning of my body. Similarly, as we understand where we fit in the church, we can work together more effectively. Our Lord needs all of us, the members of His body, to discover, develop, and deploy our spiritual gifts so the Body can function more effectively.

The third reward of discovering, developing, and deploying our spiritual gifts is that the church of Jesus Christ is edified. Did you ever notice how many times the word "edify" or "edified" appears in 1 Corinthians 14, as Paul discusses spiritual gifts? I would encourage you to note them in verses 4, 5, 12, 17, and 26. The whole discussion of perfecting the saints in Ephesians 4:11-16 would be incomplete if the results were not given, but they are. In both verses 12 and 16, we note that the church is edified. As saints do the work of the ministry, the church is edified. When the church is edified, God is glorified.

The fourth reward of utilizing our spiritual gifts is that we grow up from spiritual childhood into maturity. (See Ephesians 4:13-15.) Our goal in maturity is to attain to the "measure of the stature of the fulness of Christ" (v. 13).

One of the greatest thrills I have is seeing my young daughter, Amy, grow and mature. Regularly I see her developing new skills and talents. Daily she is growing toward maturity. What a joy it must be to the Father to see us grow into spiritual maturity.

I am certain God is not pleased when His children who ought to be teaching are still in need of being taught, are still on milk when they ought to be on meat. When His children don't grow, I am sure that God is disappointed.

One of the marks of spiritual growth and maturity is that we use our gifts for the uplifting of the body of Christ.

Finally, when we discover, develop, and deploy our spiritual gifts for use in the body of Christ, each member makes a vital contribution to the growth of the church. (See Ephesians 4:16.) It is a good feeling when we can make a worthwhile contribution to the success of any venture. One of the reasons so many Christians fall away from Christ and His church after 2 or 3 years is that they do not feel they are making any contribution to the growth and well-being of the body of Christ. It is important that each person find his niche where he can make the greatest contribution to the church.

Reflect for a moment on what would result if every Christian in *your* church were to discover, develop, and use his or her spiritual gifts.

1. Each Christian would find his place in the church.
2. All of the members of the church could work together more effectively.
3. The church of Jesus Christ would be edified.
4. Church members would grow from spiritual childhood into maturity.

5. Each member would be making a vital contribution to the growth of the church.

Many of us have started on this journey toward maturity. Christ is ahead, always leading us. It is a journey that others ought to have begun a long time ago. But the Lord has been patient with all of us. We have finally given Him our attention. He is saying, "Mobilize the forces. Let the vast army that sits in the pews week after week be trained. Join hands with each other."

We have begun. We have experienced many of the obstacles described above, but we will continue steadfastly. Won't you please join us now? I can hear Him say it one more time: "Equip the saints to do the work of the ministry . . . when this gospel has been preached in all the world, I will be back for you." Amen!